"She's proceeding to shatter the traditional political mold."
—USA Today

"She is a practical, real-life person applying the rules of everyday life to government."
—Alaska magazine

"In her first year as governor of Alaska, Sarah Palin has plunged ahead with the fearlessness of a polar explorer."
—Associated Press

"With approval ratings consistently between 80 and 90 percent, Sarah Palin is ... the nation's most popular governor."
—Bill McAllister, KTUU-TV, Anchorage

"...She has a tough-girl Alaskan résumé that most politicians could only dream of—the protein her family eats comes from fish she has pulled out of the ocean with her own hands..."
—Vogue

Governor Palin *"stands out in a state that has seen few fresh faces in politics. She is untainted by government scandal and unburdened by political debt."*
—New York Times

"In Alaska, Palin is challenging the dominant, sometimes corrupting role of oil companies in the state's political culture."
—Newsweek

SARAH

How a Hockey Mom Turned Alaska's Political Establishment Upside Down

Kaylene Johnson

EPICENTER PRESS

Epicenter Press is a regional press publishing nonfiction books about the arts, history, environment, and diverse cultures and lifestyles of Alaska and the Pacific Northwest. For more information, visit www.EpicenterPress.com.

Publisher: Kent Sturgis
Acquisitions Editor: Lael Morgan
Photo Editor: Jill Shepherd
Cover photo: Jeff Schultz
Cover & text design: Victoria Michael
Proofreader: Sherrill Carlson
Indexer: Sherrill Carlson
Printer: Lightning Source

ISBN 978-0-9800825-6-2

Hardbound Edition published in April, 2008
Trade Paperback published in September, 2008
Printed in United States of America
10 9 8 7 6 5 4 3 2 1

To order single copies SARAH, mail $15.95 plus $5.00 for shipping (WA residents add $1.90 state sales tax) to Epicenter Press, PO Box 82368, Kenmore, WA 98028. Contact info@EpicenterPress.com regarding volume discounts.

Acknowledgments

BOOKS ARE ALWAYS a collaborative effort, and *Sarah* is no exception. I'm indebted to all the people who opened their homes and hearts to share their experiences. Along with connections to the Governor, I have been profoundly moved to hear your sometimes very personal stories. For your gift of confidence, I offer my deepest gratitude.

I'd like to thank Sara Juday for an inspired meeting of the minds on a particular Sunday in October. A special thanks to Kent Sturgis for encouragement and for wise and gifted editing. A big thanks to Jill Shepherd for talented photo-editing; it's always a pleasure to work with you. Thank you and hugs to Ingrid Johnson, for help with research and other sundry duties.

And finally, to my family for your patience, good cheer, and unflagging support: Todd Johnson, Mark Johnson, Erik, Ashlee, Elias and River Johnson.

To my husband with thanks

TABLE OF CONTENTS

INTRODUCTION

SEVERAL PLOTS CAN BE FOUND in the story of Sarah Palin's unlikely rise to Alaska's highest office.

It is a political Cinderella tale in which a small-town mayor and hockey mom follows her hopes and dreams in the face of a disapproving political establishment to become the belle of the inaugural ball.

It's a version of David and Goliath in which a young populist reformer goes head to head with the good old boys and comes away still standing.

And it is a refreshingly modern can-do story about a down-to-earth woman with energy and idealism—a homemaker and mother of four—who is determined to make a difference. And she does.

Sarah's timing could not have been better.

At a defining moment, she chooses to expose the ethical lapses of the state chairman of her own Republican party, putting at risk a promising career in politics. Her call for ethics reform comes just as a legislative corruption scandal shakes public confidence. Her call for clean government resonates with a dispirited public. Soon it becomes apparent that Alaskans are ready for a change.

At forty-two, Sarah becomes the youngest governor in Alaska history and the first woman elected to the office. Her public-approval rating is the highest of any governor in the nation. She has a gift for connecting with people, possesses a steely resolve, and competes with fierce tenacity. The biggest mistake her adversaries make is underestimating her.

This is the story of how Sarah Palin pulls off the biggest political upset in Alaska history.

Chapter One
GROWING UP SARAH

> HONESTY BECAME A NON-NEGOTIABLE FAMILY STANDARD. THERE WAS AN EXPECTATION, TOO, THAT IF YOU WANTED SOMETHING, YOU EARNED IT.

SARAH PALIN'S childhood home faces Alaska's Talkeetna Mountains. In the spring, purple violets, Indian paintbrush, and wild geraniums carpet the mountains' alpine tundra in a bloom of color. In winter, the snow-covered mountains take on a rose blush in the soft alpenglow. Sarah could see these mountains from the front porch of the family's little house near downtown Wasilla. These mountains would become, like other wild places in Alaska, a place of sustenance and renewal for her boisterous and busy family.

Born in Sandpoint, Idaho on February 11, 1964, Sarah Louise was the third of four children born in rapid succession to Chuck and Sally Heath. The family moved to Alaska when

Sarah was two months old. Chuck took a job teaching school in Skagway. Her older brother, Chuck Jr., was two years old, Heather had just turned one, and Molly was soon to come. Chuck Jr. vividly remembers the days in Skagway when he and his dad ran a trapline, put out crab pots, and hunted mountain goats and seals. The family spent time hiking up to alpine lakes and looking for artifacts left behind during the Klondike Gold Rush.

"Dad never stopped lining up new adventures for us," Chuck Jr. said. The kids caught Dolly Varden off a nearby dock. Chuck Jr. loved to catch the Irish Lord, an ugly, creepy-looking fish, for the pleasure of holding it up to his little sisters' faces and making them scream.

In 1969, the Heaths moved to southcentral Alaska, living for a short time with friends in Anchorage, then for two years in Eagle River before finally settling in Wasilla. The family lived frugally. To help make ends meet, Chuck Heath moonlighted as a hunting and fishing guide and as a bartender, and even worked on the Alaska Railroad for a time. Sally worked as a school secretary and ran their busy household.

In 1974, Wasilla incorporated with a population of barely four hundred people. The Heath house sat a few blocks from the center of town, north of the railroad tracks and south and east of woodlands of birch, willow, and spruce. The woods were a wilderness playground—the kind of place where kids play out the imaginative adventures of childhood. They had a white cat named Fifi and a German shepherd named Rufus, a canine sidekick to the kids who shows up in many family photos. The children often hiked the "Bunny Trail" to the home of a distant neighbor who had kids the same age.

In both summer and winter, most of the family's activities took place outdoors. Sarah said that she appreciates the many outdoor adventures she had as a child. Fitness was a big part of family life. "My parents jumped on the bandwagon of the '70s running craze," she said. The whole family ran together, competing in five- and ten-kilometer races throughout the summer.

When the family wasn't running or hiking, it was hunting or fishing.

"We could literally go hunting out our back door," Chuck Jr. said. Sarah shot her first rabbit at age ten not far from the back porch. In her teens, she hunted caribou with her father. The family's freezer was always full of fish and game. Chuck Jr. said he didn't eat a beef steak until he was a senior in high school. Gardening helped fill the family larder.

In summer, Chuck Jr., Heather, Sarah, and Molly spent long sunny days building tree forts, riding bikes, and playing with friends. They took swimming lessons in Wasilla Lake—a pond with water so cold that they huddled around a campfire on the beach afterward to silence their chattering teeth. During the summer, their father put away the television. For entertainment, he put up a basketball hoop with a dirt court in the back yard. The Heath kids and their friends spent many hours playing ball.

Once a year, the family accompanied Chuck Sr. on a week-long class field trip to Denali National Park, where camping in view of majestic Mount McKinley left indelible memories with the Heath children.

The family often packed up and drove fifteen miles to Hatcher Pass, a scenic expanse of alpine tundra tucked between jagged peaks in the Talkeetna Mountains. In summer, the family hiked, picked berries, and followed the trails. In winter, they skied and hunted ptarmigan, an Alaska game bird.

At home, Sarah shared a bedroom with her sisters in the upper level of their wood-frame home. Chuck Jr. slept in a closet-sized room next to the kitchen. The three sisters loved listening to the patter of rain on the tin roof above their heads. The room was unheated except for a wood stove that their father installed when he built an addition onto the house. The kids had to feed wood into the stove to keep the room warm but often they decided it wasn't worth the effort to get out of bed. Instead, they snuggled deeper under the covers, watching their breath condense in the cool air.

The three sisters had a code phrase that helped ward off the chill and the scary shadows of the night. "Do you want to play Sleeping Beauty?" one of them would ask. That was the signal for Sarah, Heather, and Molly to pile into one bed for the night.

"I was afraid of everything," said Molly, the youngest. Even after Chuck and Heather left for college, Molly and Sarah slept in the same room. "I would push my bed next to Sarah's and we would hold hands, even in high school," Molly said.

One of the girls' favorite pastimes was to form clubs to organize field trips. On one occasion, for example, the group hatched a plan to hike at Bodenburg Butte, where a recreational trail overlooked the Knik River Valley. Because the Butte was too far away to bike or walk, an adult had to drive them. Sarah helped broker deals to do chores in exchange for a ride.

"One time, I remember we stacked firewood so that we could earn a ride to the fair," Molly said. But when they finished stacking an enormous pile of wood, the whole stack toppled to the ground. "We just looked at each other and got back to work."

The domestic scene in the Heath family was not without its squabbles. The children fought fiercely over the usual sibling issues and had no qualms about physically taking their differences right down to the green shag carpet. When things got out of hand, however, they agreed on one thing.

"We had a pact," Heather said. "If any of us got hurt, or if we broke something, we promised not to tell."

"We learned to toe the line at an early age," Chuck Jr. said. "If we had a problem with Mom, she'd usually just say, 'wait 'til Dad gets home.' "

Molly agreed. "Mom was like June Cleaver. I rarely remember her being upset. But when Dad came home, we stood a little straighter and turned down the volume."

Sally Heath has a kindly face and a voice that sounds like a song. Even as adults, the Heath kids enjoy listening to her voice. Sally quickly puts strangers at ease, and with smiling eyes she expresses genuine interest in everyone she meets. She is a woman of deep faith and strong convictions.

Whenever possible, Sally joined her husband in his outdoor pursuits. When he guided big-game hunts, she traded babysitting with a friend so that she could go along as camp cook and all-around assistant. She hunted, fished, cross-country skied, and ran a marathon.

Today, Sally Heath still plays an integral part in the busy households of her children, all of whom now have children of their own. When needed, she supports the working parents, volunteering as chauffer, tutor, nurse, and cook for her grandchildren. All twelve of them live in Wasilla or in nearby Anchorage.

Chuck Sr. is a wiry man, taut with enthusiasm and high-voltage energy. As a high school cross-country and track coach, he brought out the best in people around him. And he expected nothing from others that he didn't also demand from himself. During his years coaching the track team, he ran at least a dozen marathons, including the Boston Marathon.

Chuck Sr. brought his passion for the outdoors into his classroom. His classrooms then—and the Heath home now—look like exhibits in a natural history museum with pelts, skulls, and fossils adorning the walls. He continues to hunt and fish and has taken up gold mining. He often takes grandkids on a two and half hour four-wheeler ride to an old friend's mine near Gunsight Mountain.

Even in their so-called retirement, Chuck, sixty-nine, and Sally, sixty-seven, work summers for the U.S. Department of Agriculture's Wildlife Services Program. They've trapped fox in the Aleutian Islands, contributing to the recovery of bird populations decimated after the fox was introduced by Russians in the 1750s. They've used pyrotechnics to scare birds off runways in the Pribilof Islands. And they've helped eradicate rats from Palmyra Atoll, one thousand miles southwest of Hawaii. Chuck and Sally even accepted an assignment from the federal agency that took them to Ground Zero in New York City to keep rats away while investigators recovered remains after 9/11. Chuck also substitute teaches and enjoys bringing specimens from home to conduct workshops on wildlife biology.

The Heath children agree that their parents provided the right combination of affirmation, encouragement, and tough love. No infraction was more egregious to either parent than lying. Honesty became a non-negotiable family standard. There was an expectation, too, that if you wanted something, you earned it.

"We always worked," Heather said. "We never had anything handed to us."

Molly agreed. Whether weeding an enormous garden that they shared with family friends or stacking firewood, everyone pitched in. From age twelve on, everyone had a job to earn spending money—picking strawberries at the nearby Dearborn farm, babysitting, or working as a waitress at the local diner. The Heath kids knew what it meant to work.

"We knew on a teacher's salary that we would all have to pay our own way through college. We knew we'd have to be independent," Heather said.

After high school, much to her older brother's amusement, Sarah entered the Miss Wasilla pageant and won.

"I remember asking Sarah why she would enter a beauty pageant when that seemed so prissy to the rest of us," Chuck Jr. said. "She told me matter of factly, 'It's going to help pay my way through college.' "

Her family makes a point of saying Sarah was never the beauty-pageant type. Even though the scholarship she won did help pay for college, years later Sarah seemed chagrined by the pageant experience.

"They made us line up in bathing suits and turn our backs so the male judges could look at our butts," she said in a 2008 interview with *Vogue* magazine. "I couldn't believe it!"

Sarah had two childhood traits that her family says played trajectory roles in her life. From the time she was in elementary school, she consumed newspapers with a passion. "She read the paper from the very top left hand corner to the bottom right corner to the very last page," said Molly. "She didn't want to miss a word. She didn't just read it—she knew every word she had read and analyzed it."

Sarah preferred nonfiction to the Nancy Drew books that her classmates were reading. In junior high school, Heather—a year older in school—often enlisted Sarah's help with book reports. "She was such a bookworm. Whenever I was assigned to read a book, she'd already read it," Heather said.

Sarah's thirst for knowledge was nurtured in a household that emphasized the importance of education. There was never any question that all the Heath kids would go to college. With her love for newspapers and current events, Sarah majored in journalism and minored in political science. Her brother, like their father, became a teacher. Heather works for an advertising firm. Molly is a dental hygienist.

Sarah's other trait is what her father calls an unbending, unapologetic streak of stubbornness.

"The rest of the kids, I could force them to do something," Chuck Sr. said. "But with Sarah, there was no way. From a young age she had a mind of her own. Once she made up her mind, she didn't change it."

Sarah's siblings were astonished by Sarah's resolve in the face of a father whose decisions were the final word in their household.

"She never lost an argument and would never, no matter what, back down when she knew she was right," Chuck Jr. remembers. "Not just with me or with other kids, but with Mom and Dad too."

Later on, Sarah's father would enlist the help of people Sarah respected—especially coaches and teachers—to persuade her to see things his way. Yet he concedes Sarah was persuasive in her arguments and often correct. Later, when his daughter became governor, Chuck found it immensely amusing that acquaintances asked him to sway Sarah on particular issues. He says he lost that leverage before she was two.

That doesn't stop him from speaking his mind, however. During her campaigns he sometimes called to defend his daughter on talk radio. "Sarah finally asked me to stay out of it, and so I do," Chuck Sr. said. "But it hurts me when people rag on her."

Sarah's niece, Lauden, remarked that the closeness of the Heath family resembles a scene from the movie "My Big Fat Greek Wedding." When the group gets together for a holiday gathering or a sporting event, everyone is loud, opinionated, and gets into everyone else's business. The one thing they all agree on is how hard it is to watch Sarah become a target of her political foes.

"One of her strengths is being able to hold her tongue when she's been unfairly attacked," said Chuck Jr. "By staying true to her beliefs, things always seem to fall into place for her."

Not that Sarah's journey to the governor's office was easy. From the moment she began making her mark in politics, she was criticized for being too young, too inexperienced, and too naïve.

Yet, time after time over the years, underestimating Sarah always proved to be a big mistake.

Chapter Two
HEAVEN & HOOPS

> ON THE BASKETBALL COURT, SARAH EARNED THE NICKNAME "SARAH BARRACUDA" FOR HER FIERCE COMPETITIVE NATURE. "HEADSTRONG," IS HOW ONE COACH DESCRIBED HER.

THE MOST PROFOUND influences in Sarah Palin's life were gifts that she says were instilled from an early age by her mother and her father. To her mother, Sally Heath, faith in God was the most important legacy she could bestow upon her children. To her father, Chuck, sports offered an opportunity for his kids to learn the value of hard work, discipline, and teamwork.

Like her siblings, Sarah was baptized as an infant in the Catholic Church. When Sally Heath discovered what she saw as a more meaningful path to faith, her family followed her to a different church—the Wasilla Assembly of God. Sally prayed that each of her children would have a personal relationship with the God that she knew to be compassionate and merciful. With or without her husband, Sally bundled up the kids and took them to church every Sunday for morning and evening services and most Wednesdays, too. She enrolled them in church camps, vacation Bible schools, and other functions that would strengthen the values that she hoped they would embrace. Because of the time that Sally and the children spent there, the little gray church became a focal point of their lives.

As a little girl, Sarah sat through services fidgeting, staring at her shiny shoes, and smoothing her skirt. Occasionally, Chuck Jr. or Molly or Sarah or Heather would poke elbows in a sibling's ribs just to taunt one another or pass the time. It wasn't easy to be patient awaiting that sweet final hymn, after which they could go outside and play.

Over time, however, Sarah began to notice that the words being spoken from the pulpit seemed directed not just to the general congregation, but specifically to her. She found, too, that the music lifted her spirits in a way that nothing else did. And she discovered that when she prayed, she felt the presence of something far greater than herself. These were not conscious realizations so much as the gentle dawning of a child's faith. She couldn't remember a time when God wasn't real in her life. But somehow God became more than an ethereal Santa-like figure that dispensed good things to good little girls. She began to feel connected, in a soulful way, to a deep river within her, one that was fed by a power completely outside and beyond her. Sarah was growing into the legacy her mother had prayed for.

The Heaths developed many friendships through the congregational life of the church. Friends made in the sanctuary were the same ones who loudly invaded each other's homes on Friday nights. Parents played pinochle while the kids produced lively talent shows performed with great relish on the fireplace hearth. Typical of small-town living, the kids in Sarah's Sunday school were the same ones she saw daily in the classroom at Iditarod Elementary school.

When Sarah was twelve, attending Bible camp, she asked to be baptized. She wanted to make a public statement of faith, one that showed she had committed her life to Christ. On a sunny day, with Alaska's perpetual summer sunshine glittering off the chilly waters of Beaver Lake, Pastor Paul Riley immersed Sarah, proclaiming "I baptize you in the name of the Father and of the Son and of the Holy Spirit."

Sarah's siblings and her mother made the same commitment and were baptized together that day as friends and family watched from shore. It was a joyous time of celebration and reverence, a milestone Sarah never forgot. She knew, even then, that she had claimed the moral compass with which she would steer her life.

Pastor Paul Riley and his wife Helen became lifelong family friends. Paul is a lanky man with a boyish smile who retired in 1995 from parish ministry and now works as a prison chaplain. Helen wears her silver hair up in a soft bun and her round eyes dance when she talks about the pig-tailed girl who once attended their church. The church family that the Rileys created during their forty-four years at Wasilla Assembly of God continues to grow. They've taken in lost souls over the years—some of them prisoners—and everyone who meets the Rileys seems to stay in touch. When Sarah asked Paul to give the invocation at her inauguration, the couple was delighted. "We feel so proud," Helen said. "She is one of our babies."

Sarah took the commitment she made to God as a youngster seriously even through high school. She signed yearbooks with

Bible verses and held fast to the New Testament admonition from *1 Thessalonians 5:17* that said, "Be joyful always; pray continually; give thanks in all circumstances." She became the leader of the high school's Fellowship of Christian Athletes.

As her spiritual life deepened, she applied her personal brand of stubborn resolve and the Heath family work ethic to athletic endeavors. She ran on her father's track and cross-country teams and took up basketball. Chuck Sr. says that his daughter was not a gifted athlete, but what she lacked in raw talent, she made up for in drive and hard work. "In high school, she became my best distance runner," he said.

On the basketball court, Sarah earned the nickname "Sarah Barracuda" for her fierce competitive nature.

"Headstrong," is how Coach Don Teeguarden described her. "Anyone who knew Sarah would say she knew her own mind and was generally willing to express her opinion. She didn't agree just for the sake of agreement. At the time I thought those were positive attributes and I still do."

Sarah truly respected her coaches, but she had a problem. She wanted more time on the court. She knew if they would let her play, she could prove herself. But how could she prove herself if she sat on the bench during the games?

The team had a strong varsity team with several star players, tall girls who knew how to put the ball in the hoop. Sarah wasn't tall, but she was scrappy and fast. Still, she found herself sidelined as a junior and frustrated by the lack of court time. She'd already paid her dues on the junior varsity team as a freshman and sophomore and felt it was her turn to play ball.

Sarah and her friend, Michelle Carney, enlisted the help of assistant coach Cordell Randall. Would he persuade Teeguarden to let them play? Cordell replied that he would see what he could do. Then he got to thinking. Here were two good players wanting more court time. In addition to being an assistant varsity coach, Randall was coaching a JV team that wanted to win. So he talked to Teeguarden, and they agreed that the girls should play with the JV team.

Sarah was furious.

"She was so upset with me," Randall remembers. "I'm sure it was humiliating to play down. But even though she was upset, she still went out there and worked very hard." He said her face flushed crimson during every practice and Randall never knew if her face was red from the work or from anger. Sarah's one consolation was that her friend Kim "Tilly" Ketchum and sister Molly played on the JV team.

The varsity team played well that year at the state tournament in Juneau. Sarah's sister Heather, a senior, was a good player, and it seemed that Wasilla High had a shot at the state title. They had come close the year before against East Anchorage High School. Sarah was allowed to suit up and played part of the game. But in a close and dramatic championship match, Wasilla lost by two points to Kodiak High School—a fine showing but a disappointing defeat.

The next morning, coaches Teeguarden and Randall met for breakfast at a restaurant near their Juneau hotel. They didn't see the girls and wondered if they had stayed up late the night before. As the morning wore on, they began to worry. Surely the girls should have been up by then. As the coaches headed for the hotel, they saw the team walking down the street. Most of them had Bibles in their hands. The girls had gotten up early that morning to go to church.

"That's the kind of team they were," Randall said. "And Sarah was a leader in that."

In 1982, Sarah's senior year, she not only started but was co-captain of the team. In high school, all the Heath kids were selected as captains of their varsity teams.

"Dad always let us know, even if we had a great game, that we could have done a little bit more and that under all circumstances we were to remain humble," Chuck Jr. said.

Sarah rallied her team with enthusiasm and worked as hard as she'd ever worked. But she didn't always agree with her coaches.

"What we absolutely needed from Sarah was not necessarily what she envisioned when we started," Teeguarden said. "We had two kids who were very strong at the post and we were conservative about what shots we were willing to take before those two had the ball."

Teeguarden remembers that strategy wasn't popular with the peripheral players, but eventually everyone came on board. "Sarah was a great defender and her job was to make sure the ball got into the right people's hands."

In an unsettling setback, Sarah suffered an ankle injury just before the state tournament. The doctor warned that continued stress on the joint could cause permanent damage. Sarah didn't care; she wanted to play. Her father knew that a worsened injury surely would take Sarah out of sports for the rest of the year. He would lose one of his best track team members. And Teeguarden needed everything his players had to give. No matter how determined, Sarah would have a tough time playing at 100 percent. But after some deliberation between father and coach, they decided to let Sarah give it a try.

In 1982, for a third year in a row, the Wasilla Warriors won the regional championships and once again the team was on its way to the state tournament. Players like Sarah, who had come up through the ranks, were eager to go all the way.

"There was a family pride on the team. They wanted to do as well and continue the tradition of success," Teeguarden said. But would these small-town players be able to compete against Anchorage's powerhouse teams?

The team's first tournament game was against their nemesis, East Anchorage, which had humiliated Wasilla in a forty-point blowout during the regular season. Randall remembers that top-ranked East was so confident that the players casually chatted with people in the bleachers during the pre-game warm up. The Wasilla team, on the other hand, was focused like never before. The girls were not about to go down without a fight. The battle on the court that day became an epic match that no one would forget. The score was tied as the clock ticked down to the final moments. Just before the buzzer, the Wasilla girls drove for the basket and scored for an astonishing two-point victory over the state's Goliath team. Once again the Wasilla Warriors had earned a shot at the state title.

Nearly the entire town of Wasilla turned out for the championship game in Anchorage. As they did before every game, the team gathered, held hands, and took turns praying around their circle. The gym pulsated with excitement as Wasilla took to the court against Anchorage's Service High School. Teeguarden remembers their exceptional teamwork as the girls found their rhythm and passed the ball to star shooters Heyde Kohring and Wanda Strutko.

Although Sarah ignored the pain and was giving the game everything she had, Teeguarden could see her ankle was giving out. He pulled her in the second half. "That decision was tough on her," he said.

The teams continued to duke it out, with Wasilla leading most of the game but never more than a few points. Perhaps Teeguarden sensed Sarah's anguish as she watched from the sideline. Then he played a hunch: With a minute remaining, Teeguarden sent Sarah back onto the court.

In a rough and tumble drive down the court, a Service player fouled Sarah. She suddenly found herself at the free-throw line with a throbbing ankle and a Wasilla crowd going wild about the possibility of winning the state championship. Sarah dribbled the ball, held it for a second, and then took the shot. *Swish!* The cheers were deafening. Although by then she had sustained a stress fracture, Sarah iced the game by scoring her team's final point. When the final buzzer sounded, the Wasilla Warriors had won the state championship against Service High, 58-53.

Heather remembers being in college in Washington state trying to find a way to listen to the game. But in those days before live audio from the Internet and satellite radio, the best Heather could do was to wait anxiously for a phone call. "Boy, when they won, it was like I'd won too," she said.

Coach Teeguarden said that the girls showed what they were made of in that tournament. Sarah, like other players, believes basketball taught her what she needed to know about life. Teeguarden sees it differently.

"Basketball doesn't create a person, it reveals who you are," he said. "Sports, like anything we do that requires effort, provide an opportunity for growth. You find out things about yourself and sometimes you find out you have to make adjustments to become more productive and content."

Sarah mentioned basketball several times during her campaign for governor. "Basketball was a life-changing experience for me," she told a reporter. "It's all about setting a goal, about discipline, teamwork, and then success."

Perhaps it was on the basketball court that Sarah learned how to engage in combat. Sometimes the battle was not just against the opposing team; sometimes it was against the personal demons of frustration and disappointment. What she took away from basketball was not just a championship game—she came away knowing how to sharpen her focus to a razor's edge. She learned humility and the importance of surrounding herself with talented people.

Sarah learned, too, what it meant to reach deep for the resolve in the face of impossible odds.

Chapter Three
SOMETHING ABOUT SARAH

WHILE SARAH COULD LAUGH AT HERSELF, CRITICISM OF HER YOUTH AND INEXPERIENCE SPURRED HER TO PROVE SHE COULD PLAY ON ANY FIELD COMPETITIVELY.

FRIENDS SAY THAT SARAH could be anyone's neighbor, someone who might bake a batch of cookies to welcome a new family on the block or faithfully turn out on a Friday night to cheer the home football team. Her down-home demeanor is one reason why Alaskans like her.

As it turns out, during a special session she called in November, 2007 the governor did send fresh-baked cookies to the press room in the Capitol Building. And when the Wasilla football team came to compete in Juneau, she invited the entourage to dinner at the governor's mansion. To be fair, she later invited the Juneau team as well.

Sarah graduated from Wasilla High School in 1982. Tilly Ketchum has been a good friend of Sarah's since high school.

Tilly was also close to Sarah's sister, Heather, and spent a lot of time in the Heath home, a place where she always felt a part of the family.

"Sarah's no different than a lot of people that you know," Tilly said. "When she was elected mayor of Wasilla, I thought it was hilarious." After all, it hadn't been so long ago that Tilly, Sarah, and their friends had been "silly girls," learning to drive, attending proms, and trying to figure out where they wanted to go to college.

After their high school graduation, Sarah, Tilly, and two other girls enrolled at the University of Hawaii in Hilo. What better place to go to college than a tropical place with sunshine and beaches? After their arrival, however, it rained for three weeks straight. They discovered that Hilo sat on the rainy end of the Big Island and received between 130 and 200 inches of annual precipitation.

"Once we got there, we hated, it," Tilly said.

The four girls transferred to Hawaii Pacific University on sunny Oahu but homesickness claimed two of the friends who returned to Alaska. That left Tilly and Sarah sharing an apartment at the Waikiki Banyan, a block from the beach. They rode a bus to school. Sarah's aunt lived in Honolulu, offering an occasional home-cooked meal and a slice of family life. Every now and then the girls visited the set of "Magnum P.I." where they hoped to catch a glimpse of the TV show's handsome star, Tom Selleck.

Yet, a seeming paradise where they could do their homework on the beach with unlimited sunshine quickly lost its appeal. Although they were getting straight A's, the girls missed the social scene of dorm life. Surprisingly they found themselves longing for winter.

"It was always eighty-two degrees," Tilly said. "When Christmas comes around you want cool temperatures and a change of season."

The girls transferred to North Idaho College in Coeur d'Alene where they lived in a co-ed dorm with one-hundred other students and immersed themselves in a more traditional college life. Even though they were nineteen, the legal drinking age in Idaho, they didn't do anything particularly wild, Tilly recalled. Sarah once set off a fire alarm in the dorm, a prank that required a trip to the dean's office to apologize.

Sarah and Tilly took a communications class and a political-science class together. Even then, Tilly had no inkling that Sarah was destined for a career in politics. "She wasn't groomed to be in politics," she said. "All the conversations with friends and family were driven by sports."

Tilly remembers one class that required students to make a thirty-minute speech in front of a camera. Then the footage was played back for the class to critique. "It was a very scary thing," Tilly said. But apparently Sarah didn't mind the pressure of being on camera or enduring the criticism of peers.

Sarah transferred to the University of Idaho in Moscow to continue her studies in journalism and political science. Tilly stayed behind to finish a two-year program. Chuck Jr. was a running back for the University of Idaho Vandals, and Sarah enjoyed supporting her brother from the stands. Chuck was the only one of Sarah's siblings to pursue NCAA college sports but eventually was sidelined by shoulder injuries.

Throughout college, Sarah stayed in touch with her high school beau, Todd Palin. Todd was born in Dillingham, a small community in western Alaska accessible only by boat or airplane. He spent much of his childhood there. Todd's upbringing in rural Alaska nurtured his love for the outdoors and gave him an abiding respect for the land and sea. His Yupik Eskimo grandmother, Helena "Lena" Andree, was an important influence, teaching him the value of hard work and traditional Native ways. He fished with his grandparents from a young age, eventually taking over their commercial fishing operation.

"Todd loved to fish. He must be related to a fish," said eighty-seven-year-old Lena, laughing. "He was always the easiest, most soft-hearted boy. He hasn't changed except that he grew up. He's truly a family man. He and Sarah treat me like a queen."

Todd created a small-town buzz when he arrived in Wasilla during his and Sarah's senior year in high school. Everyone seemed to be talking about the new good-looking guy in school. Sarah had many male friends, but they were all boys she had grown up with. Todd was different. She first saw him on the basketball court.

"I thought he was so adorable," Sarah said. Many of the girls in class already had penned 'T O D D' across their knuckles. "So I knew I had some competition." Todd said there was never any contest. "She was the best-looking girl on the basketball team."

On one of their first dates, Todd invited Sarah and her mother to Eureka, a mountainous valley famous for its deep powdery snow. While Sally Heath cross-country skied, Todd and Sarah tore up the hillside on Todd's snowmobile. He fit right into the active, outdoor Heath family and impressed Sarah's dad, Chuck, with his athletic ability and handyman skills.

"His self sufficiency was just amazing," Sarah said. "He had a car and a truck and a job. He was a lot more grown up than most of my friends."

Todd and Sarah lived five miles apart. In the evenings they sat on their porches talking on two-way radios that Todd used on his fishing boat. "Those were the days before text-messaging," Sarah said.

Todd quickly earned the trust of Sarah's parents. When Sarah drove alone the forty-five miles to Anchorage the first time, Sally insisted that Todd lead the way and that Sarah follow in the family car, using the radios to stay in contact.

"In those days driving to Anchorage was a big darn deal," Sarah said.

During the summers after graduation and throughout college, Sarah helped Todd fish commercially in Bristol Bay. They fished from a twenty-six-foot skiff with no cabin, a boat that could carry 10,000 pounds of salmon in eight holding bins below deck. It was the most physical and dangerous work Sarah ever had undertaken. On calm days, with Bristol Bay glittering in the sunshine, the surge of migrating salmon felt like a miracle. The work was staggering, however, and on stormy days, with cold saltwater spraying the deck, it took every fiber of Sarah's resolve to stay standing.

Todd explained the importance of being in the right place and at the right time to catch salmon. "Sarah has toughed out many a cold night," he said. "Even with hundred-mile-an-hour winds, you don't want to be the one that turns back just to find out later how good the fishing was."

"Todd is a brutal boss," Sarah said. "He shows no mercy to anyone." She said Todd is nothing if not competitive when it comes to relatives and friends who also commercial fish.

One day Sarah was holding onto the rail of their fishing boat as it sidled up to a tender to which they were delivering a load of fish. As the boats made contact, Sarah's hand was smashed against a railing. She broke several fingers. Todd skiffed Sarah to shore, went back out fishing, and returned to pick her up the next day. Even with a bandaged hand she climbed back on board to help.

"I couldn't disappoint him," Sarah said. "No matter how cold or nauseous, you just didn't complain."

Chuck Sr., who later fished with Todd and Sarah, remembered one storm so bad that he and a family friend, Nick Timurphy, huddled together in a bin below deck while the young couple curled up in another waiting for howling winds and rain to subside.

"Rain was coming sideways and I wondered what the heck I was doing out there," Chuck Sr. said. "Some of the worst days of my life were spent on that boat."

Sarah did not hesitate to take on tasks usually left to the men. Sarah, her father, and Timurphy sometimes fished without Todd while he worked at his oilfield job on the North Slope. Chuck Sr. remembers Sarah driving the boat onto the trailer in dangerous surf when no one else was willing to attempt it.

Sarah graduated from the University of Idaho in 1987 with a bachelor's degree in journalism and a minor in political science. She returned to Anchorage where she shared an apartment with Heather. The day after starting her first job as a weekend sportscaster at KTUU-TV, Channel 2, she called Tilly laughing about a message from a viewer complaining that Sarah had taken the place of a male.

"It looks like you got rid of the old bum," the caller said, "And you've replaced him with a bimbo."

While she could laugh at herself, inwardly she regarded as a personal challenge any criticism about her youth and inexperience and was determined to prove she could play on any field competitively and competently.

On August 29, 1988 a light layer of snow dusted the mountain tops overlooking the Alaska State Fair in Palmer. Known as "termination dust," the first powdery snow on the peaks signaled the end of summer. Beyond the lights and laughter of the midway, Alaska's sandhill cranes were circling up to fly south for the winter.

Sarah and Todd were supposed to meet Heather and her friends at the fair but they never showed. They had decided to elope.

The magistrate at the Palmer courthouse informed the young couple that they would need witnesses for the marriage ceremony, so they walked across the street to the Pioneer Home, a state-run nursing home for seniors. Two volunteers, one of them in a wheelchair and the other supported by a walker, looked on as Sarah Heath officially became Sarah Palin.

For a time, Todd and Sarah roomed with Heather. Eventually the young couple moved into an apartment of their own. In 1989, Todd took a job with British Petroleum on the North Slope.

Meanwhile, the couple had started a family. The Palins named their first child, a boy, Track, after the track and field season in which he was born. Sarah's father jokingly asked what they would have named their son if he had been born during the basketball season. Without hesitation Sarah answered "Hoop."

Between babies, Sarah worked short stints at TV stations and at a utility company. The Palin's first daughter was born in 1990. They named her Bristol after the ocean bay where they fished. Willow was born in 1994, named after willow ptarmigan, Alaska's state bird. Their youngest daughter, Piper Indy, came in 2001. She was named after the Piper Cub that Todd flies and the Polaris Indy snowmobile Todd drove in the first of his four victories in the Iron Dog snowmobile race, a grueling 2,000-mile run from Wasilla to Fairbanks by way of Nome.

While taking care of the children and working, Sarah found time for sports and fitness. She joined an aerobics club where she formed close friendships with five other women who also were homemakers with children. The women exercised and had so much fun that they performed aerobic fitness routines at the state fair.

"We had a blast," said the group's leader, Amy McCorkell who co-owned the aerobics club. "We got free parking, tickets to the fair, and meal chits. So we'd perform, then eat our way around the fairgrounds, stop at the karaoke bar, and then go perform again."

The women got together for each other's birthdays and other special occasions. "One year, Sarah came dressed to a Halloween party as a pregnant Jane Fonda," McCorkell said. "It turns out she was pregnant with Willow but hadn't told anyone."

Despite a full schedule of changing diapers, working, keeping fit, and spending time with friends and family, Sarah felt a yearning to try to make a difference in her community.

Like her years playing basketball, she wasn't interested in sitting on the sidelines.

Wasilla Mayor John Stein and Police Chief Irl Stambaugh participated in the same step aerobics classes that Sarah attended. Stein and Stambaugh later would become Sarah's political opponents. But for the time being, it was a gathering of small-town folks who enjoyed working out together. It was this group that Sarah first approached for signatures on a nomination petition when she decided to run for the Wasilla City Council. The band of friends and fitness buffs representing all political persuasions rallied around her.

Mayor Stein could not have foreseen how this restless homemaker would send his political career into a tail-spin...

Chapter Four

SARAH TAKES ON CITY HALL

> SARAH WAS DUMB-
> FOUNDED BY THE
> INNER WORKINGS OF
> THE CITY. "RIGHT
> AWAY I SAW IT WAS
> A GOOD OLD BOYS
> NETWORK," SHE
> SAID.

WASILLA AND ITS SISTER COMMUNITY, Palmer, sit on the merging deltas of the Matanuska and Susitna rivers. Bordered by the Chugach Mountains to the south and the Talkeetna Mountains to the north, this area is known as the "Valley."

An hour's drive from Anchorage, the Valley is a casual, mostly rural place where dog mushers, farmers, homesteaders, and other independent sorts mind their own business—and expect others to do the same—and who don't worry much about government encumbrances such as zoning laws. While gaining popularity as a wholesome place—rural, peaceful, and kid-friendly—beyond the city lights of Anchorage, the Valley also developed a reputation for junky yards and cranky landowners who didn't mind using the serious end of a shotgun to run off trespassers.

In 2004, Ben Stevens, son of Alaska's U.S. senator and majority leader of the Alaska State Senate, disparagingly called people in the Mat-Su area "Valley Trash." In response, many locals wore "Valley Trash" t-shirts with pride. They didn't much care what big-city folks thought.

No matter what people said about the Valley, Sarah maintained a fierce pride in her community. She knew it was an ideal place for raising children. She liked small-town living but recognized that the area had growing pains. In the twenty years Sarah and her family had lived in Wasilla, the town had grown ten-fold from about 400 residents to more than 4,000. Many new businesses had appeared in sprawling strip malls along the city's main thoroughfare, the Parks Highway.

At the same time Wasilla was becoming a bedroom community for commuters who worked in Anchorage, it was growing as the commercial center for the Matanuska-Susitna Borough. The Mat-Su Borough, as it is known by locals, ranks third among the county-like regional governments in Alaska, both in population and physical size. At 22,683 square miles, the borough is nearly as big as West Virginia and by 2000 the borough had more than 62,000 residents.

Just as Sarah was thinking about getting involved in local politics, Wasilla City Councilman Nick Carney invited her to run for a council seat. Carney's daughter had played basketball with Sarah in high school. He told Sarah she "fit the bill" for the job. So, in 1992, for the first time, Sarah ran for public office campaigning as a "new face, new voice" who supported a more "progressive Wasilla." She was twenty-eight.

During her campaign, Sarah and Todd went door to door pulling a wagon with four-year-old son Track and two-year-old

Bristol. Many residents already knew Sarah. Others quickly warmed to her personal touch and conservative message. She won the election, defeating John Hartrick 530-310.

After taking office, Sarah was dumbfounded by the inner workings of the city government. "Right away I saw that it was a good old boys network," she said. "Mayor Stein and Nick Carney told me, 'You'll learn quick, just listen to us.' Well, they didn't know how I was wired."

Soon after her election, Sarah voted against a pay raise for the mayor. Then she crossed Nick Carney. He owned the only garbage-removal service in town and had proposed an ordinance requiring Wasilla residents to pay for garbage pick-up from their homes.

"I said no and I voted no," Sarah said. "People should have the choice about whether or not to haul their garbage to the dump."

Sarah's vote made a political enemy of Carney. She easily won a second term, defeating R'Nita Rogers 413-185, but she grew increasingly impatient with politics as usual. No matter what the issue, the entanglements of political cronyism were a frustration.

"By my second term on the council, it was apparent that things weren't going to change unless there was a change in leadership," Sarah said.

John Stein had served as mayor since 1987 and was coming up on nine years in office. Although at one time Stein had been a popular mayor, the political climate was changing. In 1994, Wasilla voters had approved term limits, but they did not deter Stein from running for a fourth term two years later. The limits did not apply to incumbents. Stein's campaign slogan was "Protect the Progress."

Sarah challenged Stein. She promised "fresh ideas and energy," vowing to replace the city's "stale leadership." She believed that instead of protecting the status-quo, policy-makers needed to be held more accountable. Too much of government was being run for the benefit of those in office.

The campaign quickly became contentious. Critics complained that Sarah, by then thirty-two, was too young and inexperienced. Her detractors claimed that she had inserted divisive party politics into a non-partisan race by posing for a photo in an advertisement with the area's Republican legislators. In an act expressing solidarity with the incumbent mayor, department heads in his administration wrote a letter supporting their boss that was published in the *Frontiersman*, the Valley's newspaper.

Even so, Sarah's conservative message resonated with the community. Nothing in the state's constitution prohibited political parties from supporting local candidates. And while she held strong convictions that aligned with the Republican platform, her first concern was for the community she hoped to serve. Like her mother, Sarah had a gift not only to make people feel at ease but also to listen to them. What were their hopes and aspirations for the future of Wasilla? If she were elected, how could she help make those dreams become a reality? Sarah had a vision for the small town. She imagined Wasilla becoming a major economic player in the state, a place where new development created opportunity and prosperity.

Throughout the campaign Sarah promised she would start trimming the budget by taking a pay cut. She promised to reduce property taxes and eliminate unnecessary government. She knocked on the door of nearly every registered voter and mailed handwritten letters to "super-voters" who had voted regularly in the previous four years.

The election grew heated with emotional letters to the editor and a searing debate in which Stein and his supporters felt the sharp edge of Sarah's competitive drive.

Wasilla voters sided with Sarah. On October 1, 1996 she defeated Stein, 651-440.

The day after the election, reporters looking for comment from the newly elected mayor found Sarah volunteering in her son's classroom. "I'd signed up to help that day and wanted to keep that commitment," she said. Seizing her mandate for change, Sarah stormed city hall, not realizing how hard it would be to make changes, especially in an administration that had become entrenched.

"Nick Carney told Sarah to her face that he'd do anything he could to make things difficult," said Judy Patrick, who had been elected to the Wasilla council. "There were some very cantankerous people on that council."

Stein's loss was a bitter one. Many of his supporters viewed the new young mayor as a kid playing a grown-up game. Police Chief Irl Stambaugh, in particular, made it clear he did not care for the new arrangement.

"I told them that I understood they had supported Mayor Stein," Sarah said of her first meeting with department heads. "But I told them they couldn't continue to support him now that he was out of office."

Sarah asked the department heads to resign and reapply for their positions. She requested resignations from the police chief, Public Works Director Jack Felton, Finance Director Duane Dvorak, and Librarian Mary Ellen Emmons. The city's museum manager, John Cooper, already had resigned when Sarah eliminated his position. The new mayor's startling demand for resignations tested the department heads' willingness to transfer their loyalties to the new administration.

"Wasilla is moving forward in a positive direction," Sarah said. "This is the time for the department heads to let me know if they plan to move forward or if it's time for a change."

During the transition, she directed department heads to get approval from the mayor's office before talking to reporters. The outraged *Frontiersman* called the directive a "gag order."

Almost as controversial as Sarah's firing of department heads was her hiring of a deputy administrator, John Cramer. The position had been vacant for eighteen months and critics asserted that the hiring proved she was not up to the job. Sarah responded by saying Wasilla's rapid growth justified filling the position.

Sarah also wrangled with the city council, which had deadlocked on filling two vacant seats on the council. Filling the vacancies required a unanimous vote of the council. In a stormy meeting, Nick Carney blocked all nominations except that of Philip Lockwood, whom he supported but who could not get a unanimous vote. Sarah announced that if the council couldn't come to an agreement, she would fill the vacant seats herself. While it was questionable whether city code allowed for such appointments, Carney backed off and the council quickly chose replacements.

All this transpired during her first two weeks in office.

Tensions ran high for several months before she eventually fired the police chief. Her action caused Nick Carney's simmering resentment to boil over. Carney, the fired police chief, and the ex-mayor formed a citizen's group called Concerned Citizens for Wasilla to discuss ousting the new mayor. About seventy people turned up for the first meeting, including Palin supporters.

According to the *Anchorage Daily News*, what followed was "two hours of sometimes raucous debate, occasionally interrupted by an incoherent man in his socks threatening to sue Carrs (a local grocery chain) and the fire marshal."

In the end, Concerned Citizens of Wasilla decided not to pursue a recall effort but instead to seek better communications with the mayor. The ex-police chief filed a lawsuit for contract violation, wrongful termination, and gender discrimination. He lost the case two years later.

Donald Moore was the Mat-Su Borough manager, an appointee, at the time. The borough did not have a full-time mayor. Now retired, the veteran manager recalled Sarah's terms as mayor, observing that there is an "inverse relationship between the size of the community and the ease of management." In other words, a small town can be hell to govern. Everyone knows everyone and lots of people have axes to grind.

"Sarah is a very gracious woman," Moore said. "But she does not suffer fools."

Almost immediately after taking office, Sarah phoned Moore, wondering about the mechanics of the relationship between the city and the borough. Her call surprised the borough manager. He explained that generally there was a guarded relationship between the city and borough governments, and that elected officials usually do not confer directly with appointed officials of similar rank.

Two-year-old Sarah clutches live shrimp caught in her father's shrimp pot in Skagway, where Chuck Heath taught school before the family moved to southcentral Alaska.

When Sarah was eight, she and her family hiked the thirty-three-mile Chilkoot Trail, camping near the 3,739-foot pass.

Sitting on a fire-hydrant box, Sarah was four or five when this picture was taken in Skagway. Lynn Canal is seen in the background.

Stuffed animal heads and fur pelts in the family's Eagle River home included furbearers such as wolverine and marten. Sarah helped her father check his trap line.

Sarah, left, and Molly displayed some spruce grouse destined for the larder. Wild game was the Heath family's meat of choice.

Chuck and Sally Heath and their four children lived for thirteen years in this small home in Wasilla. An addition was added later.

The temperature was forty-one degrees below zero when Sarah and Rufus, the family dog, posed for this picture.

Photos

Sarah, an avid reader of newspapers and nonfiction books, wore glasses by the time she was in fourth grade at Iditarod Elementary School.

Rufus enjoys a meal from his own dish during one of the family's annual outings in Denali National Park.

The "bunny trail" through nearby woods connected the Heath family home with neighbors who had children the same age.

In fifth grade, Sarah began playing the flute in the school band.
Her sister, Heather, right, accompanied her on the piano at home.

Sarah skis on Lake Lucille in Wasilla. She and her future husband later would build their home on the shores of the lake.

Photos

Sarah and her family fished through the ice for landlocked silver salmon each winter on Lake Lucille.

57

In her senior year, Sarah dated Todd Palin, her future husband. He drove this sporty Ford Mustang.

Nicknamed "Sarah Barracuda" for her fierce competitiveness on the basketball court, Sarah played on the junior and senior varsity teams in high school.

The future Wasilla mayor was Miss Wasilla in 1984. Sarah later finished as second runner-up and Miss Congeniality in the Miss Alaska competition.

Senior portraits of Sarah Heath and Todd Palin, high school sweethearts who graduated from Wasilla High School in 1982.

This photo was taken a few months before Sarah and Todd were married at the Palmer courthouse in August 1988.

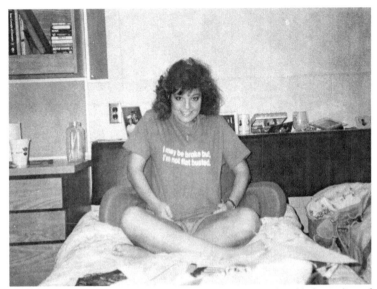

Sarah hams it up in her dormitory room at the University of Idaho, where she graduated with a degree in journalism.

Sarah attended the University of Hawaii, Hawaii Pacific University, and North Idaho College with her friend, Kim "Tilly" Ketchum, right.

COURTESY OF KIM KETCHUM

Sarah displays a large razor clam she dug at low tide at Clam Gulch on the Kenai Peninsula.

Sarah holds daughter Bristol while her father strings up a mess of Dolly Varden caught in the Wood River on a day off from commercial fishing in Bristol Bay.

"It was a very productive, non-confrontational meeting," Moore said. "Sarah's style was not scheming at all."

"Sarah's governance is consensus oriented," Moore added. "She makes sure everyone has a chance to have a say; nobody gets left out. But there comes a point when the debate is over and a decision has to be made. She's also the type of manager that once she reaches her cadence, she expects everyone to keep up."

Eventually the dust settled and a more agreeable tempo was struck between the mayor's office, the Wasilla City Council, and the staff at city hall. The *Frontiersman* softened its hard line. Vicky Naegele, the newspaper's editor at the time, said that although Palin "drove us all crazy" with the controversy she created, the paper did grudgingly acknowledge her achievements. "She grew into the position and had sense enough to surround herself with good people," Naegele said. .

It didn't hurt that Sarah began delivering on campaign promises. First, she took a pay cut, from $68,000 a year to $64,200. Second, she cut property taxes from 2 mills to 1.2 mills and eliminated personal property taxes and a business inventory tax. Third, she pushed through a $5.5 million road and sewer bond designed to attract new commercial development. Before the end of her three-year term, Fred Meyer had opened a large department store in Wasilla. The mayor also supported construction of bike paths and storm-water treatment to protect the area's lakes.

Meanwhile, John Stein wanted his job back and challenged Sarah in the 1999 election. He accused her of overspending and was especially critical of the $5.5 million road and sewer bond. Sarah countered that voters had approved the bond, convinced it was essential for growth. Stein characterized as cronyism the decision to hire as city attorney Ken Jacobus, who was counsel to the state Republican Party. Sarah reminded him that the decision to hire Jacobus was made by city council, not by her.

Sarah won reelection by defeating Stein again, 826 to 255.

Over the next two years, Sarah pushed through a temporary one-half percent sales tax increase to build a $15 million multi-use sports arena, enlisting retired borough manager Don Moore to oversee the project.

As her successes mounted, the state Republican Party took notice. Here was a young candidate who had the potential to put a new face on a party that had to carry the baggage for an unpopular president. She was attractive, articulate, and had drive. She also had a personal touch that motivated people—especially young people, undecided voters, and people who had become disillusioned with politics.

An election was coming in 2002. Frank Murkowski, who had been elected four times to the U.S. Senate before coming home to run for governor, was a shoe-in for the Republican nomination. The race for lieutenant governor was open. The party began to look at the possibilities. Some thought Sarah could offer a nice balance to the Murkowski ticket—an older, experienced man next to a focused and vibrant young woman.

What the party hierarchy did not know was that Sarah's insistence on honesty and transparency in government one day would challenge the Republican Party—an organization that had a good old boys network of its own.

Chapter Five
PLAYING IN THE BIG LEAGUES

> SARAH RAN A LOW-
> BUDGET CAMPAIGN
> FOR LIEUTENANT
> GOVERNOR. SHE
> DIDN'T HAVE A
> CAMPAIGN OFFICE, A
> CAMPAIGN MANAGER,
> OR EVEN A CELL
> PHONE.

IN MARCH OF HER LAST YEAR as Wasilla's mayor, Sarah gave birth to her fourth child. The young mayor often brought Piper with her to work, tucking the sleeping infant into a car seat under her desk.

"Being mayor was a full-time job plus," Sarah said, "Sometimes the kids would come with me. Other times, since we lived just a couple of miles away, I went home to nurse the baby. It all worked out—I just let people know I had a family."

Todd's schedule had him working on the North Slope one week on and one week off. During off weeks, he took over the household. When he was away, Sarah's sisters and mother helped fill in the gaps.

"My mom and sisters are extremely supportive," Sarah said. "I have a great network."

Even with a tumultuous beginning, Sarah had enjoyed serving as mayor. With new people on board, the city council had become less contentious. Most people in Wasilla thought she'd done what she set out to do—create positive change for their community. She also had been elected president of the Alaska Conference of Mayors, working with local, state, and federal officials on behalf of communities statewide.

Then, Frank Murkowski announced his candidacy for governor in October 2001.

Judy Patrick was serving on the Wasilla City Council as deputy mayor when Murkowski invited Sarah to run for lieutenant governor

"In those days, before all the scandals, we thought the sun rose and set on Stevens and Murkowski," Patrick said. Murkowski was a twenty-two-year veteran of the U.S. Senate. Senator Ted Stevens, the U.S. Senate's longest serving Republican, chaired the Senate Appropriations Committee, a powerful position from which he funneled billions of federal dollars to Alaska.

Sarah accepted Murkowski's invitation. She was ready to play in the big leagues. And once again, she would run as the underdog.

After Murkowski's announcement, three Republicans who had been thinking of running for governor decided to defer to Murkowski and instead seek their party's nomination for lieutenant governor. They were state Senator Loren Leman of Anchorage, a fourteen-year veteran of the legislature who was serving as Senate majority leader; Gail Phillips of Homer, for ten years a member of the state House, including four years as speaker and two as majority leader; and Robin Taylor, a former District Court judge and eighteen-year legislative veteran from Wrangell who had served both as minority and majority leader.

"There was a lot of talk about the fact that I didn't have years of experience," Sarah said. "Leadership shouldn't be based on years of public experience—it should be based on vision and example."

Sarah ran a low-budget campaign. She didn't have a campaign office, a campaign manager, or even a cell phone. Judy Patrick offered to help. In their free time, Judy and Sarah created a campaign logo and put together some advertising.

Willis Lyford, a political strategist from Anchorage, heard about Sarah from the Murkowski campaign and offered to help. Lyford had not met Sarah and saw immediately that she was not the typical contender. "She was a non-traditional Republican," Lyford said. "She was attractive, extremely attractive, and I thought to myself, this is a look you don't often see on a Republican candidate. A lot of them are overweight white guys."

After assessing the strengths and weaknesses of Sarah's candidacy, Lyford saw that the young mayor offered new energy in a field of "known commodities."

"We just needed to let people know who she was," he said. "Half the battle was awareness and visibility."

"Brilliant" was how Patrick described Lyford. "We wanted to hire him but didn't have any money. So he agreed to work for a media commission," she said.

Following Lyford's strategy, Sarah went out on the campaign trail. Lyford was right—the more people got to know Palin, the more they liked her.

"Sarah is a tireless campaigner," Patrick said. "And Todd would make a lap around the state in twenty-four hours just to put up signs."

Patrick remembered campaigning at Fairbanks at the Golden Days parade in July. A professional photographer, she agreed to meet Sarah in Fairbanks after a photo shoot in Valdez. "My client was late in Valdez and so I wound up driving all night to get to Fairbanks by four a.m.," she said. "When we got there we realized we didn't have anything to put in the parade."

Patrick phoned an acquaintance at a car dealership to ask if Sarah could borrow a pickup for the parade. The dealer was happy to oblige, handing over a shiny red pickup that matched Sarah's campaign colors.

Meanwhile, Patrick ran off business-card size copies of Sarah's picture with a short campaign message on the back. "We were so low budget. Since she's so attractive, I thought we should use our assets. Everyone wanted her picture."

Sarah chose to walk the parade route while a volunteer drove the pickup with a Palin sign in the bed of the truck. Walking gave the candidate an opportunity to shake hands and make personal connections. She carried Piper, by then fifteen months, a wriggling toddler who seemed to grow heavier as the parade went on.

"A woman came out of the crowd and gave Sarah a stroller saying she didn't need it back," Patrick said. "It was amazing how we made do with nothing and had people give us things right when we needed it most."

Back in Wasilla, Sarah discovered that the Alaska Outdoor Council had endorsed Robin Taylor. A pro-hunting group, AOC supports hunting, fishing, and trapping rights, firearms ownership, public access to public lands, and habitat conservation. Given Sarah's background as a hunter and fisher and lifetime member of the National Rifle Association, she wondered why she'd not been considered for endorsement by an organization whose activities she supported. When asked how the endorsement was decided, the council claimed to have based its decision on a questionnaire sent to all candidates. Sarah checked this with the other candidates. None remembered seeing a survey form. Angry, Sarah fired off an email of protest to AOC from her office at city hall, "There was no questionnaire," she said.

A handful of emails and a note written by her secretary thanking a campaign contributor were lapses in Sarah's effort to keep her campaign separate from city hall. Years later, *Voice of the Times* columnist Paul Jenkins dug into Wasilla city records to find the emails. Jenkins suggested Sarah had been hypocritical, comparing her lapses to conflict-of-interest scandals that later rocked the Republican Party. (The *Voice of the Times* appeared in space purchased from the *Anchorage Daily News* by VECO, an oilfield-services company. The arrangement ended after VECO's CEO, Bill Allen, pled guilty to bribing state legislators in exchange for votes favoring the oil industry.)

Sarah's race for lieutenant governor quickly became heated. In a candidate forum, Sarah highlighted her experience in politics at the local level and emphasized that being a newcomer to Juneau was an asset, not a liability. She believed the voters were desperately seeking positive, ethical leadership.

Jabbing at her opponents who originally had wanted to run for governor, she said, "I think the biggest difference between me and my Republican opponents in this race is that I'm not running for governor, I'm running for lieutenant governor."

Sarah gained in the polls as the campaign went on. But money was tight.

"We didn't have enough money and we had to allocate TV ads very carefully," Lyford said. "Related to that, we didn't have any money for polling." They could only surmise where Sarah stood from polls conducted by the better funded campaigns.

At one point, when it appeared the gap was closing, Sarah and Todd wanted to infuse the campaign with their own funds. Lyford advised them against it. "I said, 'No, you're not going to win.' The chances were very slim. It would have defied the odds," he said.

In retrospect, Lyford said that if they'd spent a little more money Sarah might have won the Republican nomination. Judy Patrick agreed. "We didn't spend a dime in southeast Alaska, and didn't campaign there at all.'"

Sarah spent $58,000 to Leman's $230,400. Surprisingly, as primary election votes were tallied, Sarah pulled ahead of Phillips and Taylor. In the end, she came within 2,000 votes and three percentage points of winning the nomination, finishing a close second to Leman in the four-way race.

Sarah believed her strong showing was a reflection of Alaska's desire for a new approach to government. "Collectively, my three competitors have served in the legislature longer than I've been alive," Sarah said. She was thirty-eight.

If Sarah was disappointed, she didn't show it. "There was no heartbreak there," she said. She believed that all things happen for a reason, and that there was a greater plan at work. She knew the direction of her next step in the political arena would become clear with time.

In the meantime, she said, "I was working full time as mayor, I'd just had Piper, we were building a house, and Todd was working on the slope."

Between the primary and the general elections, Sarah dutifully campaigned for the Murkowski/Leman ticket. After his election, one of Murkowski's first duties was to name his own successor to the vacant U.S. Senate seat. Sarah was one of at least eight people Murkowski interviewed for the vacant seat.

After weeks of speculation, the list of prospective appointees having grown to twenty-six, the governor announced his decision. He chose his daughter, Lisa Murkowski. Even though Lisa was an experienced politician who had served in the state House, her selection brought an outcry from both Democrats and Republicans protesting nepotism.

Murkowski made no apologies. "I don't think the fact that she is our daughter should preclude her from consideration based on her own individual talents, merits and proven ability," the governor said.

Sarah took a deep breath. The Senate seat wasn't the next step after all.

"That was disappointing," Judy Patrick recalled. "If he was going to appoint his daughter, why didn't he do it right away and save everyone the time, effort, energy, and speculation? There was no problem with Lisa per se, but the process."

Sarah received a call from the governor's office offering her a post in the new administration, either commissioner of the Department of Commerce or state parks director. Sarah turned down both offers. If she was going to be on the governor's team, she wanted to make better use of her skills. Then, Murkowski offered to appoint her to the Alaska Oil and Gas Conservation Commission (AOGCC), a regulatory agency that oversees the state's energy industries. Because 85 percent of Alaska's state budget is dependent on oil revenue, and 17 percent of the nation's domestic oil supply comes from Alaska, the appointment meant working at the pulse of the state's most vital industry.

Sarah accepted. "That's when the fun really started," Patrick said.

At the same time, Murkowski appointed to the commission Randy Ruedrich, chair of the Alaska Republican Party. The two appointments turned out to be a philosophical mismatch that would prove fateful in ways no one could have imagined.

Chapter Six

PIT BULL IN LIPSTICK

THE COST OF CLASHING WITH THE GOVERNOR WAS UNKNOWN. SARAH MIGHT DISAPPEAR FROM THE POLITICAL RADAR, A WHISTLEBLOWER WHOSE FAME FADED QUICKLY.

IN A PACKED GYM in the normally quiet little Glenn Highway community of Sutton, a portly man with brown hair and glasses stood to present a rudimentary drawing of how to drill a well. He assured more than two hundred fifty onlookers that tapping into coal-bed methane was as simple and safe as drilling a well for water.

The man was Randy Ruedrich, who had come to this public meeting in the Valley to address concerns of citizens who had learned that the state had leased land under their homes for coal-bed methane development, a method of extracting natural gas from coal seams.

The crowd was angry. How could the state lease out private property, and how could it happen with little advance knowledge of the property owners? Many were unaware that the Alaska Constitution reserves all subsurface mineral rights for the state. Neither the sketch nor Ruedrich's assurances changed people's moods.

"It was a ridiculous drawing, like something a kindergartener would have come up with," said Kathy Wells, director of Friends of Mat-Su, a watchdog group monitoring land-use issues in the Mat-Su Borough. "It didn't matter if you were Democrat or Republican or a tree hugger, or whatever—you touch someone's very soul when you lease out land without the owner's knowledge."

Aside from opposition to gas-field construction and concern about possible contamination of the water supply in Sutton's residential neighborhoods, there was outrage that the state seemed to be acting in the best interests of everyone but the private property owners. No one seemed to know who Ruedrich was representing—the state, or the developer, or both. Why was he supporting the controversial proposal when his job as a member of the Alaska Oil and Gas Conservation Commission was to regulate the oil and gas industries? Was his support for the development a conflict of interest?

Mat-Su Borough residents weren't the only ones wondering. Sarah, who chaired the commission and served as its ethics supervisor, had received complaints about Ruedrich not only from people in the Valley but also from commission staffers who protested that Ruedrich was conducting Republican Party business from his commission office.

"Every month she had to sign a piece of paper that said there were no ethics violations on her watch," said Judy Patrick, who often met Sarah for lunch in Anchorage. "She just couldn't sign that paper. So she reported it."

What followed was a deafening silence.

In an interview with the *Daily News*, Sarah explained that she first sought help from Murkowski's chief of staff, Jim Clark. It took three weeks for Clark to respond, at which time he told Sarah, "I'll handle it."

A few days later Sarah told Ruedrich that he should expect a call from Clark. "Oh yeah, he called me, he calls me every Sunday," Sarah remembers Ruedrich saying. "He asked me if I was doing anything wrong. I told him no."

Meanwhile, the *Daily News* reported, Sarah discovered that the commission did not have ethics-disclosure statements from Ruedrich. Under the Executive Ethics Act, all state employees must disclose possible conflicts to their supervisor. It turned out Ruedrich had given his ethics statements to Sarah's boss, Kevin Jardell, assistant commissioner of administration. Jardell, an attorney, had stayed for several months in Ruedrich's home while he did legal work for the Republican Party. Although the statements should have gone to Sarah, Jardell signed off for Ruedrich, writing that his "outside interests are not incompatible or in conflict" with his state employment. Never mind that Ruedrich was chair of the state Republican Party. Never mind that he still was receiving deferred compensation from previous employers including British Petroleum and Doyon Drilling—companies under investigation for alleged environmental violations on the North Slope. Or that he was acting as an arbiter in a dispute between two drilling companies.

As the coal-bed methane issue simmered in the Valley, Ruedrich's actions within the commission were creating tension. First, he talked about looking up the political affiliations of each staff member with the intent of "getting" anyone who had served in the previous administration of Democratic Governor Tony Knowles. He appeared to be claiming travel expenses to attend Republican functions. And he seemed to have a personal vendetta against the commission's attorney, Bob Mintz, whom Ruedrich described as a "liberal Democrat" even though other commissioners found Mintz scrupulously neutral and non-partisan in his work.

In response to complaints, the *Daily News* reported, Sarah made more than a dozen contacts up the chain of command reporting Ruedrich's questionable behavior. She tried counseling Ruedrich. Nothing changed. If the good old boys network at Wasilla City Hall had been a challenge, this network was in a league all its own.

"She was eaten up that no one was doing anything," Patrick said. "She was consumed by a wrong that needed to be made right. She couldn't stand it—she never forgot whose money it was or that she was working for the public. Being accountable was a big deal, and in this case no one was being held accountable."

Chris Whittington-Evans, president of Friends of MatSu, attended a public meeting at which Ruedrich displayed slides demonstrating the purported safety of coal-bed methane production. Whittington-Evans had seen them before. He had attended a breakfast meeting where representatives of Evergreen Resources Inc., the coal-bed methane developer, had used the same slides to promote its agenda.

Later, it was discovered that Ruedrich had e-mailed a confidential AOGCC memo to Evergreen Resources Inc.'s lobbyist Kyle Parker. Emails showed that Evergreen Resources had indeed sent images to Ruedrich before the Sutton meeting.

The *Daily News* also reported that Ruedrich worked with Parker's law firm behind the scenes on legislation that favored coal-bed methane development.

"He was undermining all the work of AOGCC's engineers, scientists, and statisticians," Sarah said. "It was unfair to all the staff members who were working hard to do their jobs."

Whittington-Evans sent an e-mail to Sarah demanding Ruedrich's resignation. He wrote, "Mr. Ruedrich's continued service calls into question the purpose and credibility of the AOGCC as well as its ability to act in an unbiased way to protect and conserve the resources of the state. Aggressive lobbying in favor of developments he obviously doesn't fully understand and continued use of his office in improper ways to press forward his agenda and that of the Republican Party reduce the commission to an ineffectual, biased body the public cannot trust."

Sarah agreed. She also was getting calls from legislators who wanted to know what was going on, and asking who was in charge. The credibility of the AOGCC and her own reputation were at stake. She forwarded the email to Jim Clark, Attorney General Gregg Renkes, and Mike Miller, the commissioner of administration.

Two days later, Randy Ruedrich resigned.

Sarah told reporters she was instructed by Assistant Attorney General Paul Lyle to hack into Ruedrich's computer to look for evidence that Ruedrich had broken state ethics laws. She printed out dozens of incriminating e-mails and documents. But even though Ruedrich was gone, it wasn't clear whether the Murkowski administration was conducting a formal investigation.

Sarah couldn't get a straight answer from anyone, including Attorney General Gregg Renkes, who claimed that confidentiality provisions of the state ethics law prohibited him from confirming that a complaint had been filed or that an investigation was underway. The *Daily News* accused the Murkowski administration of "stonewalling," asserting that the attorney general was playing a legal shell game to avoid release of potentially embarrassing information.

Meanwhile, Sarah was told simply to continue her inquiry, keep her findings secret, and deny media requests for information.

The public, especially people in the Valley, wanted answers. Her staff at the AOGCC office was getting nervous. To Sarah, the whole thing smacked of a cover-up and she wanted no part of it.

She wrote a letter to Murkowski demanding that either the state explain that she had been under orders to remain silent, or that she be allowed "to handle this issue the way I deem is most appropriate." If the issue is ignored, she warned, "I will take such further action as I deem appropriate to protect my reputation with regard to this unfortunate matter."

The following week, Paul Lyle, the assistant attorney general, began an investigation, but did not acknowledge that an investigation was taking place. No one even acknowledged receipt of the evidence Sarah was sending.

In protest, Sarah resigned from the commission a month later. Even then, she continued to receive letters at home from the Department of Law ordering her to remain quiet.

"One of the most offensive things was realizing why they thought I was on the commission," Sarah said. "They thought I'd be a good soldier and try to climb the political ladder."

Her resignation did not end the matter. On February 27, the assistant attorney general produced a sixteen-page ethics complaint against Ruedrich but refused to make the document public. The *Daily News*, Associated Press, and KTUU-TV went to court seeking access to emails, documents, and other public records reflecting Ruedrich's activities on the AOGCC.

Ruedrich and the press reached an agreement that resulted in Ruedrich offering his side of the story and making public the documents that were being kept secret. Ruedrich also negotiated a settlement of the ethics claims against him. The *Daily News* reported that in this agreement with the state, Ruedrich admitted to violating three of four alleged ethics violations—misusing his official position by engaging in partisan activity, improperly disclosing a confidential legal document to a lobbyist, and conducting partisan political business from his state office. He was fined $12,000, the largest sum ever paid for ethics violations in Alaska. Sarah was vindicated.

Murkowski said little except to grumble that the media was to blame for the scandal. He praised Ruedrich for being a "survivor."

Chris Whittington-Evans praised Sarah's actions as risky and courageous. "At the core was a sense of right and wrong," he said. "It came at a politically interesting time and gave her the opportunity to set herself apart."

She may have set herself apart, but Sarah now found herself sitting on the bench again. She knew she had gambled her political future. But she trusted everything would work for the best as long as she stood up for the truth. She welcomed the opportunity to spend more time with family and signed up as a volunteer for Track's hockey team. She continued running and began training for a marathon. And while she was sidelined because she had bucked the political establishment—the governor and the head of the Republican Party—she watched with interest as the public's dissatisfaction with the Murkowski administration continued to grow.

Some state legislators were fed up, too. Among them was Rep. Eric Croft of Anchorage, who was especially critical of Gregg Renkes, a close friend of Murkowski. Renkes had managed the governor's campaign. Once elected, Murkowski appointed Renkes as attorney general, even though his friend had not practiced law in Alaska.

Croft questioned Renkes' ties with Colorado-based KFx Inc. Renkes owned more than $120,000 worth of KFx stock and had personal ties to the company's executives. Renkes had negotiated the terms of a multi-million-dollar international trade deal that would export coal from Cook Inlet to Taiwan, using KFx's patented coal-drying process. The trade deal stood to benefit the coal-technology company, and its stock was being traded actively throughout the negotiations.

The governor was under increasing public pressure to investigate allegations of Renkes' conflict of interest. Under state law, complaints of ethics violations by the governor, lieutenant governor, or attorney general are to be investigated by the Alaska State Personnel Board. Instead, Murkowski asked former U.S. Attorney Robert Bundy to look into the matter. Bundy's report concluded that Renkes' stock in KFx wasn't significant enough to be considered an ethics breach, but that he had violated state ethics laws by not seeking an outside opinion on his involvement in the Alaska-Taiwan coal deal.

In response, Murkowski issued a perfunctory letter of reprimand to his friend but did not ask for his resignation. A number of legislators complained that the letter was a slap on the wrist, and Representative Eric Croft decided to file an independent complaint to the personnel board.

Croft, a Democrat, said, "I wanted it to be bi-partisan, and Sarah already had a reputation for standing up against corruption. I wanted her to know going in what the risks were. She just said, 'Fine, what do we do next?'"

Croft's complaint asserted that conclusions in the Bundy report were in error. Using previous precedent, Bundy had determined 1 percent of a company's holdings to be a benchmark for determining conflict of interest. Renkes' $120,000 worth of stock in KFx totaled only 0.02 percent of the company's shares, Bundy said, and was therefore "insignificant" under Alaska law.

"To most Alaskans, this defies common sense," Croft said. "If an employee only owns 1 percent of Exxon, they still have a $3 billion conflict."

Murkowski was furious at Croft and Sarah for resurrecting what he considered to be a closed matter. His spokeswoman accused them of catering to their own political ambitions. And Murkowski's chief of staff wrote that they were "trying to hijack the report . . . and create a sideshow."

In her toe-to-toe face-off with the governor, Sarah once again refused to back down. She fired off a guest-opinion piece to the *Daily News*. "It's said the only difference between a hockey mom and a pit bull is lipstick," she wrote. "So, with lipstick on, the gloves come off in answering administration accusations."

After slamming Murkowski for "hiring his own counsel, paid for by the state, to investigate his long-time friend, confidant, and campaign manager," Sarah concluded by writing, "Despite those in Juneau who think otherwise, it's healthy for democracy to ask questions. And I'll bet there are hockey moms and housewives all across this great state who agree."

Two months later, Renkes resigned.

Recalling the chain of events later, Croft observed that when confronted by the ethically challenged Murkowski administration, Sarah might have taken a couple of different approaches. She could have said, "Who am I to question the big boys?" or "The only way to get ahead is to play the game."

"She rejected both of those," Croft said. "She was not naïve and I had no sense of political calculation. The conversation always came back to standing up for what's right."

The political fallout remained to be seen. On one hand, Sarah could disappear from the political radar, a whistleblower whose flash of fame faded without the party support.

Yet, she did not fade into obscurity. The public sat up and took notice. People were becoming angry.

A hockey-mom with pit-bull tenacity might be just what the state needed to clean up its act

Chapter Seven
FRANK MURKOWSKI'S DOWNFALL

WHEN THE GOVERNOR APPOINTED HIS DAUGHTER TO THE U.S. SENATE, 50,000 ALASKANS SIGNED PETITIONS FAVORING AN INITIATIVE REQUIRING ELECTIONS TO FILL FUTURE VACANCIES.

FRANK MURKOWSKI'S FALL from grace was almost as spectacular as his resounding election victory in 2002 when he received 70 percent of the vote in the Republican primary election. After twenty-two years representing Alaska in the U.S. Senate, Murkowski came home amid statewide optimism that he would move Alaska toward a positive and prosperous future.

"For the first time, in a long time, there is unity in the House and Senate not only in Juneau but in Washington as well," Murkowski said at his inauguration at Centennial Hall in Juneau on December 2, 2002. "Never before have the stars been so in alignment."

Yet, almost from the beginning, there were complaints that Murkowski ruled more like a monarch than an elected leader. When he appointed his daughter to the U.S. Senate, outraged Alaskans quickly proposed a citizen's ballot initiative requiring future vacancies to be filled by a vote of the people. One in twelve Alaskans—50,000 people—quickly signed petitions. In 2004, voters approved the initiative and it became law without the signature of the governor.

Murkowski then proposed a statewide sales tax that the legislature flatly rejected. In response, the governor slashed popular state programs including the long-revered Longevity Bonus for senior citizens. The program, which began in 1972 and was being phased out, provided payments to a maximum of $250 a month for seniors who had turned sixty-five by 1996. Elders across Alaska were dismayed by the broken promise of a state that had pledged to help them make ends meet during their twilight years.

"We must take responsibility for prioritizing what our governments can do based on what we can afford," Murkowski said.

Thus when the governor proposed acquisition of an executive jet for his official travel, many Alaskans were incredulous. Murkowski first tried to get a $2 million grant from the U.S. Department of Homeland Security. The federal government refused the request. Then he went to the state legislature, asking for $1.4 million to lease a jet. He said he was trying to upgrade the state Department of Public Safety's fleet of aging turboprops. In addition to being available for his own travel, Murkowski told lawmakers, the jet could be used in emergencies and would be available to fly Alaskan inmates to a private prison in Arizona. Reacting to widespread public opposition, legislators denied Murkowski's request.

The governor did not give up. He secured a line of credit and went shopping for a jet. The state signed a contract in the summer of 2005 to purchase a Westwind II, complete with cream leather furniture, burgundy carpeting, a stereo system, and a flush toilet. On top of the $2.6 million purchase price, the state paid $97,600 to train four pilots and $95,000 for repairs and upgrades.

In retrospect, Sarah was glad she had not been elected lieutenant governor.

Chapter Eight
A FAMILY DECISION

SARAH BELIEVES THAT EVERY LIFE HAS A HIGHER PURPOSE. SHE HOLDS THAT LIFE'S MEANING IS FOUND IN SERVING SOMETHING LARGER THAN ONE'S SELF.

IN 2004, FRIENDS AND SUPPORTERS urged Sarah to challenge Lisa Murkowski. Sarah had made a name for herself as a reformer, and supporters thought she had a good chance of winning. So, Sarah approached her family to discuss the possibility. Like all of her decisions to run for office, the decision had to be unanimous.

"People don't believe me, but it's true. It had to be a family decision," she said. Todd was up for a move to Washington, D.C. and the girls were on board as well. But son Track, in his early teens, was becoming aware of the contentiousness of a political battle. He valued his privacy, and felt uncomfortable in the limelight. "Track did not want me to run, and he was adamant about it. He had to bless me," Sarah said. "If he had said at the time 'This is great,' I would have done it."

When Sarah declined to toss her hat into the ring, some political observers speculated that she was weary of bucking the Republican establishment. "That wasn't true either," she said. "It was a family decision. In the end, all you can do is hope the message, the truth, will be received in the manner it was intended."

Yet Sarah continued to feel drawn to public service. And she continued to follow reports of Governor Murkowski's political blunders. During the time between Sarah's resignation from the AOGCC and her bid for governor, Sarah had embraced her role as a hockey mom, organizing hockey benefits, helping with school events, and volunteering in the community.

"As fulfilled as I was with four kids, I knew something was missing," she said. "It wasn't a dark time, but there was confusion. Was there something else I was supposed to be doing? I spent a lot of time in prayer about that."

Sarah believes that every life, not just her own, has a higher purpose. She holds that life's truest meaning is found in serving something larger than one's self. When she gives high-school commencement addresses, she always encourages young people to find and follow their destinies.

Meanwhile, Sarah's children were growing up. Track planned to attend a high school out of state to play hockey. Bristol and Willow were coming into their own, playing sports, and growing close to their cousins and extended family as they sought to find their own places in the world. And Piper, the youngest, was ready to enter elementary school.

As the 2006 governor's race approached, both friends and distant admirers called on Sarah to run against Frank Murkowski. Her brother Chuck assured her the time was right. Other people, such as John Reeves in Fairbanks, had read about Sarah's work on the AOGCC and how she'd busted Randy Ruedrich for ethics violations.

"I called and said, 'Listen, I want to help you win this,' " Reeves said. A land speculator and miner, Reeves told her "I'm one of those rare Democrats—one with money." Sarah was attending a hockey tournament in Fairbanks and agreed to talk to Reeves in the bleachers while watching the kids play. "I knew from the moment I met her that she was going to win," said Reeves, who switched parties in order to support Sarah.

"So many people from all walks of life came together and said, it doesn't matter what party, Sarah is what we want," Reeves said.

Sarah said she would think about running. Meanwhile, she wondered who else might run. "I was waiting for someone to come forward, but I only saw people who represented the status quo," she said. "There were no new ideas or energy and no new blood."

Willis Lyford, the political strategist who had helped run her campaign for lieutenant governor, was one of the few who discouraged her from joining the race. "I told her she didn't have the experience. I told her it's going to hurt when these guys came banging around about her lack of experience. It won't be fun and it won't be pleasant." He suggested she make an easy run for lieutenant governor. It would give her some on-the-job training. Besides, she was young; she had lots of time.

Yet, Sarah's resolve was growing. There was no time like the present. This time, when Sarah talked with her family about running, the decision was a unanimous decision to go for it.

Sarah announced her long-shot bid for the governor's office on Alaska Day, October 18, 2005, at her home in Wasilla. Little did Sarah know that surprise events ahead would propel her into serious contention.

Ten days after her announcement, another controversy brought negative attention to the Murkowski administration. Murkowski had fired from his cabinet Tom Irwin, commissioner of natural resources. Irwin had written a memo questioning Murkowski's closed-door negotiations with oil companies about developing a natural-gas pipeline. Addressed to the governor's chief of staff and the state attorney general, the memo suggested that Murkowski was offering the oil companies too much and it questioned the legality of the negotiations.

In response to the firing, six senior staffers in the Department of Natural Resources resigned. People who knew Tom Irwin said he had not taken the commissioner's job for personal gain, but for the opportunity to serve Alaska.

All six letters of resignation said, "I regret that I have to take this action, but I have no alternative following the dismissal of Tom Irwin as commissioner of the Department of Natural Resources."

Murkowski's "A-team" for the gas pipeline negotiations was gone, but concerns about what the exodus might mean for ongoing gas-line negotiations were dismissed by the governor. "We're losing some qualified people," he said. "But as we all know in life, people come and go. And we will find other people to replace them."

Meanwhile, the public was growing increasingly angry. As the primary election neared, polls showed Murkowski's public-approval rating had dropped to as low as 15 percent.

Bill McAllister, a correspondent for KTUU news in Anchorage, called the timing of Sarah's candidacy "Sarah-dipity. "There could not have been a bigger contrast between Murkowski and Sarah in terms of political tone," he recalled.

"I had a bet with my colleagues at work—a high-end single malt scotch with one and a fine bottle of wine with the other—that Sarah would win the primary."

Chapter Nine
A SIMPLE PROMISE

> THE OLD GUARD DIDN'T KNOW WHAT TO MAKE OF THE YOUNG POPULIST CANDIDATE, ESPECIALLY WHEN SHE BEGAN MOVING UP IN THE POLLS.

"I'LL LISTEN."

Those two quiet words from Sarah Palin were barely heard over the heated exchange between the two men who loudly interrupted one another and ignored the moderator's pleas for a civilized discussion. The setting was a televised debate among Republicans in the three-way race for their party's nomination for governor. The primary election was three weeks away.

Governor Murkowski and challenger John Binkley, a Fairbanks businessman, largely ignored the attempts of John Tracy of KTUU-TV to keep the conversation on course.

As the nasty exchanges continued, Sarah's voice, no longer quiet now, rose over the others—clear as a bell in a boxing ring. "You know what, you guys?" she said. "We owe Alaskans a better discourse than this."

Taken aback, Murkowski, Binkley, and even the moderator looked at Sarah for an instant as if the school principal had just served notice on the playground bullies. Both candidates quieted and the discussion continued in a more orderly fashion. Sarah stressed that Alaskans were tired of obsessive partisanship and special interests tearing the state apart. "If you want good public service you have to put the people of Alaska first," she said.

It was one of many moments during the campaign when Sarah trumped her rivals with a simple appeal to common sense. Her authoritative presence in that debate demonstrated that Sarah was not the political lightweight that some detractors claimed.

Sarah trusted that Alaskans could think for themselves without the sanction of a party "machine." She believed that the state needed fresh energy to forge a new culture in state government, a culture without secret deals favoring special interests made in the bar of Juneau's Baranof Hotel.

There were times when seasoned politicos groaned at Sarah's populist image. In one TV commercial, she swung five-year-old Piper up onto her hip. In another, she jogged alongside Bristol. Pundits wondered when she planned to polish a more executive image. After all, she was playing the big leagues now.

Still, Sarah was young, energetic, articulate, and attractive. Like many Alaskans, she hunted caribou, fished for salmon, and embraced an independent Alaska lifestyle. She played the political game the way she had played basketball at Wasilla High School, with passion and drive. She doggedly stood up for her beliefs. And one of those beliefs was that Alaskans deserved better than what they were getting from their current governor.

The low-budget, grass-roots campaign did not faze Sarah. The campaign was so frugal that volunteers built "Palin for Governor" signs using dismantled wooden crates used for shipping snowmobiles.

Kris Perry, who later became Sarah's campaign manager, and her husband Clark, worked tirelessly. "While other candidates were sending out glossy flyers, we sent out stuff that I made at home on my computer and printer," Kris Perry said. Kris had been president of the Wasilla Chamber of Commerce when Sarah served on the Wasilla City Council in the early 1990s. Clark had known Sarah since high school.

On the campaign trail, Sarah didn't make promises she couldn't keep. At one meeting with a group of trawlers and processors on Kodiak Island, Sarah listened but respectfully disagreed on a particular issue. Volunteer Frank Bailey recalled that before wrapping up the meeting she told the fishermen, "At this point I'll understand if you decide to support my opponent. Regardless of that, if I become governor I want you to know that I respect your views and will continue to listen to your concerns."

The next morning, back at Anchorage campaign headquarters, the fishermen's group called asking for two large eight-foot "Palin for Governor" signs to display in Kodiak. "We've decided to support Sarah because we believe she'll listen," the caller said.

Volunteers came from all walks of Alaskan life—hunting guides, teachers, dog mushers, restaurant workers, retirees. These were everyday people who had volunteered their time and efforts, not to protect a special interest, but to support an ideal. Many never had been involved in a campaign and others were so weary of and cynical about politics that they'd dropped out—until they met Sarah. Most relished taking on a deeply entrenched good-old-boy network. Sarah was not wealthy. Her husband was a working man. Nor was she politically connected. Her father was a teacher, her mother a school secretary.

Frank Bailey was one of Sarah's first campaign volunteers. He had recently taken a management buyout from his job as a contract manager at Alaska Airlines to be a stay-at-home dad to his daughter Kaia and their soon-to-be-born son, Devin. Bailey looked at the field of potential candidates and became discouraged. Wasn't there someone out there who would take a stand for integrity in government?

Then he remembered reading about Sarah Palin. He'd never met her, but he'd read newspaper reports about how she'd stood up to Randy Ruedrich and later, the state attorney general. So he emailed Sarah, encouraging her to run for Governor. When she announced her candidacy, he picked up the phone and asked, "What next?" Sarah told him to show up at a vacant downtown office in Anchorage with paintbrushes and Windex.

Bailey decided that Sarah represented a new vision and a higher ideal in state government. He said people were always asking "Is she for real?" A reporter from the *Juneau Empire* called Bailey at one point asking who was backing this "rebel" candidate. The reporter had identified "big oil" as Murkowski's supporter and the travel industry as Binkley's—so who was behind Sarah's campaign? Bailey's answer: "everyday Alaskans who want a fair shake."

The grassroots effort suited Sarah just fine. She did not intend to become beholden to anyone. There were times when individuals representing large corporations offered big checks to her campaign and she just smiled and shook her head. "Thanks so much, but really, I just need your vote." If they wanted to help, she added, would they mind setting up a few yard signs in their neighborhoods?

She also turned down a few checks from people she knew couldn't afford to spend the $100 they were offering the campaign. "All I need to win the race is your vote," she assured them.

Meanwhile, the old guard didn't know what to make of the young populist candidate, especially when she began moving up in the polls despite their best efforts either to discredit her or support her opponents.

"Anyone who was part of the establishment fought against her. [Talk show host] Dan Fagan clawed, fought, ridiculed, embarrassed, and deliberately misrepresented Sarah," Bailey said. Disparaging remarks on radio programs sometimes backfired. Fagan showed up at the Palin campaign headquarters one morning to clarify a point before his daily show. Waiting at the front desk was a man who took one look at Fagan and dug out his checkbook. "This is your fault," he said, waving his checkbook in the air. "Every time you bash this woman on the air, I'm down here writing out another $500 check. Cut it out."

Two weeks before the primary election, the Republican Party held a picnic at Kincaid Park in Anchorage. Randy Ruedrich and Bill Large, the party's attorney, decided that the event should be "non-partisan"—no active campaigning would be allowed during the picnic. Matthew Peters, who helped plan and promote the event, said nothing to that effect had been discussed at any of the planning meetings he attended. At every other Republican picnic, people wore campaign t-shirts and carried signs for their favorite candidates. That was the whole point. Why should this picnic be different?

Wearing what was described as a "sea of red Palin t-shirts," Sarah's campaign volunteers and supporters showed up. A few carried yard signs. Spirits were high as they ate hamburgers and enjoyed the summer afternoon. However, the presence of the red shirts was like waving a flag at an angry bull. Bill Large stormed out of the Kincaid Park chalet and confronted a Palin group standing on a sidewalk. Witnesses said he was trembling with rage.

Large demanded that Sarah's campaign leave the area. "Why?" asked Matthew Peters. Large roared back that the rules had been broken. Peters' father, an attorney, stepped in and asked for a copy of the rule. Large took a file folder he was carrying, tore it down the middle, and proceeded to hand-write a "rule" and shove it at one of Sarah's supporters.

"I reminded Mr. Large that the Constitution reaffirmed 'the right of the people peaceably to assemble' and that he had no authority to order a peaceful group of citizens to remove themselves from the public sidewalk," Peters said. "I also invited Mr. Large that if he had a problem with people standing on a sidewalk, he should call the police."

Large's temper erupted. Witnesses said he shoved a seventy-year-old woman wearing a Palin t-shirt. She pushed back with a Palin sign that said "Take a Stand." Large shouted that the Palin group was a bunch of Nazi "brown-shirts" and "communists." Then Ruedrich joined Large in asking the group to leave. When Sarah came over to see what the trouble was, she touched Large's arm lightly to introduce herself. "Don't touch me," he said.

Large later expressed regret for the incident and apologized. But the nasty confrontation solidified Sarah's reputation as an outsider shunned by Republican Party leaders. She refused to play ball on their terms and it was making them crazy.

Running on a cornerstone of ethics and transparency in government, Sarah made good on McAllister's bet, pulling off the biggest political upset in state history. She defeated Frank Murkowski, winning 51 percent of the vote to 19 percent for the incumbent in the three-way primary. Her victory attracted national attention. Wasilla's small-town hockey mom had taken a stand against a powerful political establishment and won.

On election night, Sarah's supporters gathered in the ballroom at the Captain Cook Hotel. Every time new results were posted favoring Sarah, a rousing cheer rose up. When it was apparent she was going to win, Sarah and four-hundred supporters walked together the four blocks to the state election headquarters in the Egan Center, waving red Palin signs and chanting "Sa-rah! Sa-rah!" while passing motorists honked their horns.

"It was so exciting. It's hard to describe—it was just electric," said Joann Smith, a long-time supporter who thinks back on that primary parade as one of the most memorable moments of her life.

With just three months before the general election, Sarah's growing band of grass-roots volunteers and supporters had their work cut out for them. But their energy and enthusiasm soared.

More than Sarah Palin's stance on any particular issue, the message that moved Alaskans was Sarah's simple promise: "I'll listen."

Then, a shocking political scandal rocked the state.

On August 31, the FBI raided six legislative offices, revealing the existence of a broad federal criminal investigation into alleged statewide corruption.

Bill Allen, CEO of the oilfield-services company VECO, and the company's vice president, Rick Smith, the next year pled guilty to charges of bribery and conspiracy. They admitted to making more than $400,000 in payoffs to lawmakers to win passage of an oil-profits tax favorable to the oil industry. Lobbyist Bill Bobrick also pled guilty to conspiracy for bribing a lawmaker while representing a private prison company. Four legislators were arrested. Later, the FBI served a search warrant on the Girdwood home of U.S. Senator Ted Stevens and questions arose over the campaign practices of Congressman Don Young.

Overnight, ethics reform became a hot issue in the general election campaign. Whether it was "Sarah-dipity," good luck, exquisite timing, or Divine Providence, the prospects suddenly looked much better for the reform-minded maverick Republican who vowed to be an agent of change.

Chapter Ten
ELECTION 2006

SARAH FOCUSED ON OPENNESS AND, TRANSPARENCY AND UNWAVERING COMMITMENT TO THE ALASKA CONSTITUTION. SEAN PARNELL BROUGHT TO THE TICKET A WEALTH OF EXPERIENCE.

WHEN SEAN PARNELL AND SARAH stood on the stage together after winning the Republican primary election, Parnell realized he didn't know Sarah Palin very well.

"As my wife said during the campaign, 'You don't know who your dance partner is going to be'," recalls Parnell, who had won his party's nomination for lieutenant governor and would be Sarah's running mate in the general election.

Parnell came from an old-guard Republican family. His father, Pat Parnell, had served on the Anchorage Assembly and later in the Alaska House. The younger Parnell was elected to the House in 1992, serving two terms before winning a seat in the state Senate in 1996. Unlike Sarah, he was well-regarded by the Republican Party.

Parnell took a break from politics after growing cynical in his work in the legislature. "I was starting to suspect the motivations of the people around me," he said. Six years later, with "a renewed personal faith," he returned to politics "full of hope for Alaska's future again."

The day after the August election, Sarah and Parnell sat down to discuss the campaign ahead. Numb and tired from campaigning, they must have felt a little awkward at that meeting, like a couple on a blind date.

Parnell remembers being stunned by the reality of the situation. He estimated that $1.5 million would be needed to win. At that point, he and Sarah had $60,000 between them. They had no support from the Republican Party, which could have given them up to $200,000 but did not. Although three campaign signs hung in the window of the party office in Anchorage, Sarah and party chair Randy Ruedrich were not speaking. Sarah called for Ruedrich's resignation as party chair. Ruedrich refused to step down. At the Republican Party booth at the state fair in Palmer, supporters were told that Palin campaign materials were "not available."

Looking at their bleak finances and lack of party assistance, Parnell wondered if they would be able to attract volunteers. As it turned out, he recalled later, "That should have been the least of my concerns."

What Sarah and Parnell shared from the beginning was a sense that they were part of something more profound than personal politics or campaign strategy. That realization forged the beginning of trust between them.

"It wasn't about Sarah, and it wasn't about me. It was about something bigger. We knew that for this to work, it would have to be through hands greater than ours," Parnell said.

Volunteers showed up in large numbers. Volunteer coordinator Mark Fish said an estimated 1,200 volunteers worked on the campaign statewide, not counting hundreds of people who worked independently on behalf of the candidate.

The challenge was how to channel their energies and enthusiasm constructively. Most had no campaign experience. "It was like herding cats," Fish said.

Contributions began coming in, too, though ultimately the campaign would spend less than the Democratic nominee, Tony Knowles. Funded almost entirely by individual Alaskans, Sarah's campaign cost $907,000 compared to $1.3 million spent on the Knowles campaign. Yet, surveys showed Sarah holding a 17 percent lead early in the general election campaign and she was making her opposition nervous.

Tony Knowles and an independent candidate, Andrew Halcro, accepted invitations to twenty-five debates and forums in forty-five days. Their strategy was to wear Sarah down and expose her as a political lightweight.

"Knowles and Halcro felt the more they could debate her, the better they'd do," recalled Bill McAllister. The Democrats wanted to pin her down on the particulars of public policy. "She deflected all that stuff," McAllister said, "and they were frustrated that she wouldn't participate."

In her typical style, Sarah refused to play their game. Rather than sell her positions on specific issues, she sold herself as a new voice for Alaskans.

Sarah likened herself to a quarterback, drawing on the strengths of individual players. "When they get out there and they read the defense and see that the circumstances are changing, that quarterback has to call an audible and has to be able to communicate with key players," she said.

She said her positions were clear: She was running as a fiscal conservative, a reformer, and an advocate for the people of Alaska.

"I'm offering Alaskans what our state needs and that's a new governor with new energy, with a vision for change, for integrity, for prosperity and for success," she said.

Knowles and Halcro jumped on every opportunity to discredit Sarah, chiding her for being a "no show" at some candidate events. In one instance, Sarah declined a forum invitation so that she could attend a send-off for troops being deployed from Fort Richardson to Iraq. Parnell went in Sarah's place. Given three minutes to make a statement, he explained that his running mate had chosen to be with the men and women who were putting their lives on the line in service to their country. She wanted to support their families and trusted that the audience understood the importance of thanking the troops for their sacrifices. Parnell told the audience that Sarah looked forward to future discussions about raising the bar in Alaskan government, and that she hoped she would have an opportunity to serve Alaskans as their governor.

McAllister remembers that Knowles was visibly upset. Sarah's choice to spend time with the troops lifted her above the fray. Whether she intended it that way or not, Sarah had won the debate without even being there.

At another forum, the Knowles campaign rolled out a four-year plan for education. When it was Sarah's turn to speak, she paid tribute to her father as a beloved school teacher and promised—without specifics—to make education a top priority.

"The Knowles camp was apoplectic," said Bill McAllister. "They couldn't figure out why the media wasn't all over what a twit she was."

Knowles ran a well-oiled, polished campaign. He issued press releases almost every day, produced sophisticated commercials, had a top-notch website, and called on Alaskans to trust his experience. He campaigned hard and cashed in the political capital he had earned during two terms as governor.

In contrast, Sarah's campaign chugged along through the efforts and enthusiasm of less experienced volunteers. One such volunteer was Kerm Ketchum. With a shock of white hair and deep blue eyes, Ketchum was a crusty Alaskan, a retired Air Force computer whiz who once taught computer science at the Mat-Su branch of the University of Alaska. His family had been friends with the Heath family ever since Ketchum's daughter Tilly had played basketball with Sarah. Despite lack of political experience, Ketchum believed in Sarah's integrity and knew it was time for change.

"You know that claim that Sarah had a political machine?" Ketchum said, laughing. "Well, myself, Frank Bailey, the Perrys, and Kathy Fredericks—we were it."

Frank Bailey said a big challenge was dealing with misinformation. Sarah's opponents wrongly insisted she had accepted money from outside groups, pointing to commercials placed on Sarah's behalf by the Republican Governors Association, which interjected itself into the campaign without first contacting the Palin campaign.

"Another big one was that she was anti-Native, which was ridiculous. She's married to a Native. We campaigned with Todd's grandmother, Lena," Bailey said. "People from communities like

Kotzebue, Dillingham, King Salmon, the Interior and Unalakleet rose up and went after people who were in error—namely the Knowles camp."

Sarah also was accused of standing against Alaska's big three oil companies—ConocoPhillips, BP, and ExxonMobil. "We had to strike a balance between countering misinformation and giving credence to something not deserving of attention," recalled Kris Perry, Sarah's campaign manager.

Halcro, the independent candidate, was a former legislator and owner of a car-rental business in Anchorage. He continued to insist that Sarah was a political lightweight. In one debate, Halcro asked Sarah if she knew what percentage of the state budget went to constitutionally mandated services.

Because Sarah did not give a percentage, Halcro sarcastically replied, "Sarah, I didn't hear an answer to my question, so let me repeat it to you, and I'll say it slower." Sarah responded that as a candidate she expected trash talk from her opponents but she hoped he didn't treat his customers so disrespectfully.

At a Rotary Club forum, Halcro goaded Sarah about the price of oil after she talked about how Alaska was in a good position with oil prices at nearly $58 a barrel. Halcro corrected her. "From what I understand," he said, "oil closed yesterday at $53 and change, but you know, what's $5?"

"He's the smartest boy in the room," Sarah said later. "He always knows everything."

As the general election neared, Sarah's lead in the polls began to narrow as executives of some of the state's largest corporations including ConocoPhillips, GCI, Providence Health Systems in Alaska, and Northrim Bank rallied around Knowles. Several major newspapers endorsed Knowles, including the *Anchorage Daily News*, the *Sitka Sentinel*, and the *Juneau Empire*.

Parnell recalled that their campaign strategy shifted toward the end. "Initially we pursued a strategy to go separately to cover more ground. We finally concluded that our strengths were better communicated together."

Sarah focused on openness and transparency and her unwavering commitment to uphold the Alaska Constitution. Parnell brought to the ticket a wealth of legislative experience and experience in natural resources, budget, financial, and legal matters. When they appeared together, they came across as a composed and confident team. And they reminded voters that Knowles had his chance to build a natural gas pipeline during his eight years as governor.

Ten days before the election, Dittman Research and Communications reported Sarah leading by just 1 percent. However, 10 percent of those polled were still undecided. Of Alaska's 465,000 registered voters, 115,000 were Republicans, 66,500 were Democrats, and 33,500 voters were affiliated with other parties. By far the majority of voters—250,000—were independent, and it appeared they would decide the outcome.

By the time voters went to the polls, Sarah's poll numbers were up again, by a few percentage points. It looked like the outcome would be close.

Once again, Sarah's campaign filled a ballroom at the Captain Cook Hotel on election night. Cheers went up as results from precinct after precinct favored Sarah. In the end, the results were not close. Sarah won 48 percent of the vote. Tony Knowles finished with 41 percent and Andrew Halcro was a distant third with 9 percent. As it had after the primary, the jubilant Palin crowd marched down Fourth Avenue to claim victory at the state election headquarters in the Egan Center.

In the end, McAllister said, the election was about the candidate rather than a campaign.

"Ultimately no one cared which forums were attended or what policy paper was put forward. It didn't matter. Sarah was the right person at the right time," he said. "The huge irony of the 2006 election is that she couldn't have won it any other way. Between quitting the AOGCC over Randy Ruedrich, her platform of ethics coming in the midst of an FBI investigation, and anti-incumbency sentiment of the voters, she was inevitable—unbeatable."

Perry said Sarah took her win in stride. "You'd think someone would get all puffed up and proud after winning an election like that," he said. "But with Sarah, the greater the responsibility, the more humble she became."

Parnell said the election ushered in a new age of politics in Alaska.

"It's the first campaign in Alaska history that was truly a people-driven, people-oriented campaign" he said. "In a world where representative government was shaken by corruption, people took power back into their own hands."

Chapter Eleven

FOR SUCH A TIME AS THIS

We the people of Alaska, grateful to God and to those who founded our nation and pioneered this great land, in order to secure and transmit to succeeding generations our heritage of political, civil, and religious liberty within the Union of States, do ordain and establish this constitution for the State of Alaska.

—Preamble, Alaska State Constitution

> CHUCK HEATH SAID WATCHING HIS DAUGHTER AND SON-IN-LAW COME DOWN THE AISLE WAS ONE OF THE MOST MOVING MOMENTS OF HIS LIFE.

ALASKA'S CONSTITUTION TOOK EFFECT when Alaska became the 49th state on January 3, 1959. It had been drafted by fifty-five elected delegates who gathered at the University of Alaska in Fairbanks during the winter of 1955-56.

With a sense of historic purpose, the delegates hoped to create a solid foundation for statehood and to convince Congress that

Alaska possessed the political maturity and natural resources necessary for self-government. Alaskans were weary of the federal government and outside corporations—mainly the canned salmon industry and mining interests—controlling the territory. They wanted the old guard out and a new, representative government to take its place.

Fairbanks was chosen to host the convention so that delegates could draft a constitution far from politics as usual in Juneau and away from the influence of lobbyists.

Fast forward fifty years, to December 4, 2006. With a sense of historic significance, nearly four thousand took their seats at the Carlson Center in Fairbanks to witness Sarah Palin's inauguration as governor.

For the first time since statehood, the inauguration would be held somewhere other than Juneau. To commemorate the 50th anniversary of the ratification of Alaska's constitution—a document she vowed would be her guide in the years ahead—Sarah chose Fairbanks. In honor of their vision for Alaska, Sarah invited the last living delegates to the constitutional convention. Jack Coghill, Vic Fischer, George Sundborg, Seaborn J. Buckalew, and convention clerk Katie Hurley joined Sarah's family seated on the stage. Nearby were Lieutenant Governor Sean Parnell and his family, former governor Walter Hickel, and other dignitaries.

About 2,000 school children arrived in buses from Fairbanks and surrounding communities to witness the event.

Everyone else making their way into the Carlson Center that day were the people that Kerm Ketchum called "Sarah's Machine." Kerm recalled that at first he had to convince his wife Gina and one of his daughters that Sarah could handle the job plus raise a family.

"They couldn't support her at first because of her kids," he said. "I have four daughters and guess I'm the women's-libber around here. I convinced them she would find a way."

A few seats down from the Ketchums sat Clark Perry. He'd been in charge of merchandise for the campaign including t-shirts, bumper stickers, bracelets, and hats. He staffed the phone and did whatever needed doing. Sometimes he played tic-tac-toe with Piper to keep her entertained. For months he had volunteered after work from his job as a cook at the prison in Sutton. He drove forty-five miles each way to Anchorage, worked into the night, then drove back home to Wasilla. Later he stayed home with two young sons while his wife Kris ran the campaign.

"The campaign started with nothing, not even a file cabinet," Perry said. "Sarah worked out of her car and a wicker bag—not even a briefcase. And yet there we were, sitting with people who fifty years earlier had signed Alaska's constitution. I mean, I'm just a cook, and I was sitting next to military generals, watching Alaska's first woman be sworn in as governor."

Nick Timurphy sat in the audience too. A Yupik Eskimo from Dillingham, Timurphy grew up with Todd and recently had taught Bristol to drive the boat and set nets in their fishing operation. Commercial fishing was a family tradition that he and the Palins looked forward to passing on to the next generation. When he wasn't fishing, Timurphy worked at the local hardware store and coordinated Dillingham's Food Bank. Timurphy took time off to fly from Dillingham to Anchorage where he met up with a friend for the six-hour drive to Fairbanks. Before leaving Anchorage, they stopped to buy Nick a suit.

"I'd never worn a suit in my life before that," Timurphy laughed. "I felt a little out of place at first, but that went away with all the excitement."

Was he surprised that Sarah had become governor? Not really, he said. "Sarah's a smart girl and like anybody else, she set her mind to it and did it."

Lydia Wirkus took one of several buses that carried Wasilla residents to Fairbanks for the inauguration. When she arrived, she pitched in by handing out programs and directing people to seats that were quickly filling. It had been almost six months since the day she rode her bike from her home in Chugiak to Sarah's campaign headquarters in Anchorage to volunteer for the campaign.

Eighty-nine year old George Williams, who also rode the bus to the inauguration, had taken it upon himself to be a one-man stumping campaign for Sarah. He traveled all over the Mat-Su Valley in a 1997 Chevy pickup truck with a large campaign sign attached to the tailgate. Every day, he tracked down one of the many friends he had made in fifty years and told them why they should vote for Sarah. Williams had come to Alaska in 1957 and went to work operating a steam shovel at the Mrak Coal Mine in Sutton. Over the years, he'd worked as a heavy equipment operator and a construction contractor, and had helped establish a statewide vocational training center. The inauguration was one of the high points of his life, Williams' daughter, Wendy Garwood, said at her father's funeral several months later.

A rousing bagpipe band marched into the auditorium announcing the arrival of the new governor. Sarah and Todd (who quickly became known as the "First Dude") smiled

Governor Palin and daughter Piper hauled provisions to an elderly gold miner, a family friend, in the Talkeetna Mountains in 2007.

Chuck and Sally Heath, the governor's parents, and their extended family in December, 2007.

The Palin girls with their fraternal great-grandmother, Helena "Lena" Andree, and fraternal grandmother, Blanche Kallstrom.

Sarah and daughter Piper.

Sarah fishes on Lake Lucille.

Palin supporters campaign at a busy intersection in Anchorage.

Chuck and Sally Heath learn that their daughter would be the Republican candidate for governor in the 2006 General Election.

The *Anchorage Daily News* proclaims Sarah's election as Alaska's 11th governor and the first woman to hold the state's top office.

Sarah and her family bow their heads during the benediction at the new governor's inauguration in December 2006 in Fairbanks.

JOHN HAGEN/FAIRBANKS DAILY NEWS-MINER

Sally Heath keeps an eye on Piper during the inauguration.

Juneau's Centennial Hall hosted one of four Governor's Balls held throughout the state. CHRIS MILLER/CSM PHOTOS

Governor Palin and her family in an official state portrait
ALASKA GOVERNOR'S OFFICE

Sarah was elected mayor of Wasilla at age thirty-two.

Sarah and daughter Piper.

Photos

Bristol Palin helps her mother serve hot dogs and hamburgers at the 2007 Governor's Picnic in Anchorage.

Sarah runs her section of a fifty-mile relay footrace over the Hatcher Pass Road in the Talkeetna Mountains.

The governor visits a pipeline training event run in part by the Plumbers and Pipefitters Union Local 375 in Fairbanks with Brian Quackenbush and Jim Laiti.   LANCE PARRISH

Jerry "Bones" Grauf, a family friend who mines gold in the Talkeetna Mountains, was a staunch supporter of Sarah in her race for governor.

The governor visits the 1st Stryker Brigade at Fort Wainwright, where she was briefed on how the troops are trained.

ALASKA GOVERNOR'S OFFICE

The governor and daughter Piper, center, share Russian tea and cookies with Nancy Hakari's third-grade class at Riverbend Elementary School in Juneau.   ALASKA GOVERNOR'S OFFICE

Sarah hauls in a net full of salmon. She once broke several fingers in an accident while fishing from the boat.

CHRIS MILLER/CSM

Commercial fishing comes naturally to Sarah, whose family spent a lot of time fishing, hunting, and camping. CHRIS MILLER/CSM

The governor waves the checkered flag at the finish line of the 2007 Tesoro Iron Dog snow machine race in Fairbanks.

ERIC ENGMAN/FAIRBANKS DAILY NEWS-MINER

Sarah congratulates Todd after he and his teammate win the 2007 Iron Dog snow machine race.

ERIC ENGMAN/FAIRBANKS DAILY NEWS-MINER

broadly as they walked together toward their parents. Chuck Heath said watching his daughter and son-in-law come down that aisle was one of the most moving moments of his life.

Libby Riddles, the mistress of ceremonies, took to the podium. In 1985, she became the first woman to win the Iditarod Trail Sled Dog Race. Sarah said that while other college students put up posters of pop stars in their rooms, she hung pictures of Riddles.

"She was bold and tough," Sarah said. "Thank you for paving the way."

Sitting in the area reserved for Alaska's mayors, Curtis and Linda Menard remembered Sarah as a little girl growing up in Wasilla. Their son, Curtis Jr., had been Sarah's good friend since childhood and Track's godparent. Her friend's unexpected death in an airplane accident was one reason for Sarah's conviction that there is no time like the present to find your place in the world. The Menards knew their son would have been proud to have shared this moment.

Sarah's siblings sat nearby, marveling at how someone as down to earth as Sarah could reach such extraordinary heights by standing firm for her beliefs. "She has the drive, the dedication, and the faith to make it happen," Molly said.

At the podium, Sarah welcomed her family. "To my family, our big family, I love you. Y'all cleaned up real well today. I don't see a Carhartt in the bunch," she joked.

In her inauguration speech, Sarah vowed, "I will unambiguously, steadfastly, and doggedly guard the interests of this great state as a mother naturally guards her own, like a nanook defending her cub."

She spoke of moving forward to develop Alaska's natural resources not only to make possible a secure future for Alaska but also to lead the nation in its energy planning.

"America is looking for answers. She's looking for a new direction. The world is looking for a light. . . .that light can come from America's great north star. It can come from Alaska."

She promised that discussions about a natural-gas pipeline would begin immediately with Alaska's three big oil companies—ConocoPhillips, ExxonMobil, and British Petroleum—and that she also would invite to the table other companies such as TransCanada, MidAmerica, Shell, and Chevron. She pledged the negotiations would be open and transparent.

She challenged Alaskans to hold her accountable. "And right back at you," she told the crowd. "I'll expect a lot from you too."

Sean Parnell spoke earnestly about tackling Alaska's social ills including domestic violence and substance abuse. "This vision of Alaska— of safe homes and streets, excellence in our schools, of families together in peace, and for dignity in our twilight years—rests securely in hands larger and more capable than our own. However, we cannot simply wait and watch events unfold. Every one of us must own this vision of Alaska's future. We must take responsibility for the things we can change. With new energy and new vision, Governor Palin and I will lead by seeking to replace Alaskans' fear and despair with hope and opportunity."

John Reeves, the land speculator who during the campaign had painted an excavator to look like a dinosaur chomping on the "old boys club," watched the ceremony from the back.

"Although several of the dignitaries and VIPs sitting up front invited me to join them, I sat in the cheap seats with the folk that actually voted for her," he remembered. "Many [seated in the front rows] were the Republican party faithful that fought Sarah tooth and nail the whole campaign. It was actually kind of funny. . . . Sarah knew how she got where she was and her speech reached out to the nosebleed section where we all sat and enjoyed the ceremony and what we had accomplished."

After the swearing-in ceremony, the crowd erupted in raucous applause, foot stomping, and chanting of "Sa-rah! Sa-rah! Sa-rah!"

At the end of the ceremony, blue and gold balloons rained down from the ceiling. The Palin family followed the bagpipers out of the Carlson Center.

Little Piper Palin, wearing a bright red dress and a tiara, held her mother's hand as they walked smiling into the cold December snow.

EPILOGUE

ONE OF GOVERNOR SARAH PALIN'S first tasks was to deal with the tangle of issues left by Frank Murkowski during his final days in office.

One hour before his term expired, Murkowski appointed thirty-five people to various state boards and commissions. One appointment was that of Murkowski's son-in-law, Leon Van Whye, to the board of the Alaska Railroad. Murkowski also named his chief of staff, Jim Clark, to the board of directors of the Alaska Natural Gas Development Authority, a board with which Clark had had contentious relations during the administration's failed negotiations for a natural-gas pipeline.

Governor Palin quickly rescinded Van Whye's and Clark's appointments. "We'll keep the good ones" she said. The governor also re-hired several of the "Magnificent Seven," the officials of the Department of Natural Resources who had resigned en masse when Murkowski fired DNR chief Tom Irwin

In another parting act, Murkowski pardoned Whitewater Engineering Corp. of Bellingham, Washington, a company that pled no-contest to criminally negligent homicide in the 1999 avalanche death of one of its workers, 46-year-old Gary Stone. The company had a history of work-safety violations in Alaska before the conviction. Stone's family learned of the pardon only after the fact, when reporters called for comment.

Within weeks of taking office, Palin signed into law a bill requiring governors to notify victims in advance of pardoning convicted felons. "In a perfect world, this bill wouldn't be necessary," she said. "It's just very unfortunate that we have to put into law something that should be common sense for a governor."

Palin immediately put Murkowski's jet up for sale on eBay.

She also called a special legislative session in an effort to remove the taint of corruption over a Petroleum Profits Tax (PPT), a deal brokered behind closed doors by Governor Murkowski. As an alternative to PPT, she proposed a bill known as Alaska's Clear and Equitable Share (ACES), which restructured the way oil companies are taxed. As a result, the legislature increased the base oil-tax rate from 22.5 to 25 percent of profits.

Palin also signed into law the Alaska Gasline Inducement Act (AGIA), which created a competitive bidding process for companies wanting to build a natural-gas pipeline from the North Slope. As an incentive, the state offered $500 million in seed money for the project.

With the price of oil edging toward $100 a barrel and the new oil-tax structure in place, the state projected a $4.6 billion surplus over the next two years. Before proposing her first budget, Palin consulted Alaskans directly, asking in a survey how best to spend the state's expected windfall. A *Newsweek* article called Palin's style "a pragmatic, post-partisan approach."

In the ongoing federal criminal investigation, Republican legislators Vic Kohring, Pete Kott, and Bruce Weyhrauch were arrested on charges that they accepted bribes to support legislation for VECO Corp., an oil services company. The company's top officials, Bill Allen and Rick Smith, pled guilty to bribing lawmakers with cash or the promise of jobs in exchange for their votes. In a separate federal case, Republican state Rep. Tom

Anderson was prosecuted on seven counts including bribery for taking money he thought was coming from a private prison firm. Lobbyist Bill Bobrick also pled guilty to conspiracy in the scandal.

On the same day Anderson was convicted, Palin signed an ethics-reform package that closed loopholes and tightened the rules on what compensation legislators could receive from outside interests.

The federal investigation moved forward. In a March, 2008 plea deal with federal prosecutors, Jim Clark, chief of staff to former Governor Murkowski, pleaded guilty to felony conspiracy charges for arranging an illegal $68,000 campaign donation from VECO to pay for consultants and polls in support of Murkowski's 2006 re-election campaign. Prosecutors said that Clark used his position and the Office of the Governor to advocate an oil tax rate favored by VECO.

During Palin's first year in office, she withdrew state support for the proposed "bridge to nowhere" from Ketchikan to its airport on Gravina Island. The $398 million project was to be supported by a Congressional earmark that became a national symbol of pork-barrel spending. She redirected the federal funds to the state Department of Transportation for other projects. She said it was time for Alaska to "grow up" and to contribute to the nation rather than freeload from the federal government.

Not all of her decisions were popular. She vetoed hundreds of millions of dollars from a public-works budget, and she postponed closure of the Matanuska Maid Dairy, a state-subsidized dairy that eventually went belly-up. There was concern, too, that both the tax increase on oil profits and the AGIA gas-line bidding process would discourage oil companies from investing in the state.

Parnell recalled the administration's first day in their Anchorage office. He and Palin were taking a look around and came to the door that joined the governor's office with the lieutenant governor's office, a door that had remained mostly closed during the four years of the previous administration. Palin looked at Parnell, propped the door open and said, "Do you mind if we keep this open?" Parnell said it was a significant moment that reflected how they would work together as a team

Bill McAllister said the first legislative session after Palin's election was the least acrimonious session he had seen in seven years as a capitol correspondent. The second session was less peaceful. Yet, a year and a half after taking office, Governor Palin continued to enjoy high approval ratings.

Meanwhile, Todd and Sarah Palin surprised Alaskans in March 2008 when they announced that the governor was seven months pregnant with their fifth child. Trig Paxson Van Palin arrived on April 18, one month early. The name "Trig" has two Norse meanings— "true" and "brave victory" while Paxson is the name of an Interior lake popular among snowmachiners. Early testing revealed that the baby would have Down Syndrome. In a statement, the family said, "Trig is beautiful and already adored by us . . . we feel privileged that God would entrust us with this gift and allow us unspeakable joy as he entered our lives." Todd Palin, the "First Dude," took a leave of absence from his job as production operator on the North Slope to help with the household.

One of Palin's first acts in the Governor's Mansion was to lay off the chef. She figured her family could spare the expense to the state. The family always had managed just fine without one. She has a driver, but often drives herself. She enjoys the few private moments she spends in the car. To stay fit, she continues running, which she prefers to do alone.

Epilogue

While her security detail scrambles to keep track of the governor, the rest of her staff knows that no matter what, her kids come first.

"She can be on the phone with Dick Cheney and have (state Senate President) Lyda Green right outside her door, and her kids call and she goes, 'Oops, hold on,'" Sharon Leighow, Palin's deputy press secretary, said in an interview with *Alaska* magazine. "Her kids trump everyone, and I think that's pretty neat."

Writing in the *Anchorage Daily News*, Steven Haycox, professor of history at the University of Alaska Anchorage, suggested that a popular governor is remembered long after leaving office even if popularity is not necessarily a measure of a governor's accomplishments and historical importance.

Haycox believes that Palin will be remembered with the same kind of respect and affection accorded Bill Egan, Alaska's first governor, who had an uncanny capacity for remembering names, and Jay Hammond, the "reluctant politician" who championed the Alaska Permanent Fund.

Sincerity, an authentic concern for people, and a commitment to democratic process, Haycox wrote, "usually engenders respect, a full hearing, and more often than not, affection."

Going to the grocery store with the governor to pick up a gallon of milk is like shopping with a movie star, according to her sister Molly. Everyone wants an autograph. Everyone wants to share their thoughts with a governor who can hardly resist the opportunity to connect with everyday people like her.

Sarah Heath Palin is at heart a sister, a daughter, and the little girl who learned how to work hard, stand up for herself, and never tell a lie.

APPENDIX

Surely the warm heart of Alaska is in the Carlson today. I thank you so much for that toasty welcome. This is an honor. Welcome, all.

To our state constitution framers, we honor you. Past and present officials from across the land, we're grateful for you. I thank all our former governors who have served, all of them. And to my family, our big family, I love you. Ya'll cleaned up real well today...I don't see a Carhartt in the bunch.

Especially to all you students, thank you for skipping school. Thank you for being here.

I am so glad you all are here, and Libby Riddles—first woman to win the Iditarod. When I was a college student outside in the 1980s, my roommates plastered their dorm walls with pictures of Madonna and Magic Johnson and Metalica. Adorning my walls, truly inspirational, were pictures of Libby Riddles. She was an underdog. She was a risk-taker, an outsider. She was bold and tough. Libby, you shattered the ice ceiling. Thank you for plowing the way.

I am humbled to be here with so many good Alaskans in the land of great Native heritage. Alaska is a family. And Alaska Natives, you're the first family. Your embrace welcomed newcomers to this frontier yesterday. It lets us move forward in unity today with respect, with good stewardship of the land of your birth. We're blended. Let us be united with one heart.

Fifty years ago here in Fairbanks, at the Alaska Constitutional Convention, those wise providential pioneers gathered, wrote, and birthed the newest, biggest, richest-in-resources state in the union with the document that shall guide me as governor.

It demands that Alaskans come first. It will keep my compass pointed true north. It's the tool to build Alaska with strength and with order. Their brilliant document, the constitution, is austere. It concentrates clearly on resource development for our people, and is eerily prophetic. Today although we stand on the threshold of a new frontier, these pioneers still speak to us from the past.

At the start of the convention, delegate Bob Bartlett said he saw two distinct futures for Alaska—one of wise resource management leading to wealth and industry, the other of servitude stemming from loss of control over our resources leading to despair. They had a choice of which route to go as we do today—regress or progress. There's no part of the world where the people and the land fit as they do here. Our nature resources are our life blood and are commonly owned by all of us. We are unlike any other state in the union.

Here, the people are in charge. We have rights and responsibilities to produce. Done right, we see vitality, we fund services, we make a more secure America. And we see opportunities for jobs, for work, and that should be our goal because man was created to work.

Our founding documents then were shaped to fulfill promises that we be self-sufficient and self-determined with a special understanding of the relationship of Alaska and her people to her lands and her water and her wildlife. Bartlett instructed those delegates, saying, "This moment is critical in history. The future and well-being of our present and unborn citizens depend on wise administration of these developmental activities."

Bartlett was warning against being exploited by outside interests because we were so resource rich. He said, "The taking of our resources without leaving a reasonable return to support needed services will mean a betrayal in the administration of the peoples' wealth. The danger is that competing interests determined to stifle development here which might compete with activities elsewhere will acquire our lands in order to not develop it until such time as, in their omnipotence in pursuit of their own interests, they see fit. If our opportunities are squandered, the people of Alaska may be even more the losers than if the land had been exploited."

Wow, the state of the state being what it is today as we embark on gas-line negotiations tomorrow, Bartlett's words spoken nearly a decade before I was born could have just as easily been the content of this morning's newspaper editorial. So, understanding the gravity of that warning, fifty-five heroes wrote strong and clear powers into our state's fine blueprint. It's that ink that will guide me in taking Alaska boldly toward our birthright.

I will unambiguously, steadfastly, and doggedly guide the interests of this great state as a mother naturally guards her own— like a southeast eagle and her eaglet, or more appropriately here in the Carlson, like a nanook defending her cub. Our state, our lands, our future are in our hands.

The most important issue today, as Lieutenant Governor Sean Parnell said, is developing energy supplies, building the foundation upon which we will progress our role internationally. Central today are natural gas needs. We must tap reserves and explore for more to energize our homes, our businesses, for new industry to come alive, to heat our economy, and allow us self-sufficiency while gifting our nation with domestic supplies. Couple this with ANWR oil and inexhaustible alternative energy sources. Alaska can lead the nation in a much-needed energy plan to secure these United States, to create a safer world. Why not Alaska fueling the nation? Why not Alaska leading the world? These are perilous times in our world.

America is looking for answers. She's looking for a new direction. The world is looking for a light. It's Governor Hickel who reminded me that "that light can come from America's great North Star—it can come from Alaska." It can happen only if we work together in true partnerships and work with our legislators, not against them, putting aside political pettiness and crushing corruption. This is our opportunity to show a new direction.

We can show a new direction, and we can inspire the world. So, I take with me tomorrow our constitution to gas-line negotiations and work with global partners and independents to market our gas. We're in a position of strength here but that strength comes not from my hand; it comes from what I hold in my hands. Let's be vigilant with competing interests if they encroach on our sovereignty or divide us or force us from opportunity.

We've learned lessons about competing interests. Sometimes it's involved our own federal government. Take fishing, a quick example. First, we'll manage wildlife for abundance—enough for all. I need Alaskans, though, working together when federal decisions adversely affect us. Regions, races, user groups, gear groups must unite in battle for Alaska's right to harvest and to develop. Robust fishers should revitalize coastal communities left in the wake of allocation decisions that mirror fishing issues from fifty years ago that kept us beholden to outside interests when we lived under federal orders that favored a privileged few.. So, we sought statehood to control our resources and for fairness. Not going backwards, I oppose contradictions to competition and free enterprise that hurts Alaskans.

Our constitution explains all this—wildlife, oil, gas, minerals, timber, and access for our maximum benefit. Alaska is vast enough for all, plus tourism and technology and university research—all means of creating honest prosperity. We've got great opportunity today even with changes on the national scene. With our

Congressional delegation in the minority right now, obviously we must prudently consider state priorities as our relationship with federal funding streams change. Don't fear, though, perhaps delayed dollars coming in. Instead, let's make our wealth out of the wilderness and make our living on the land and on the water. Let's use our hands to build and our minds to lead the nation in innovative advancements.

Governor Hickel said he "never feared an economic depression so much as a depression of the spirit." This is a time to be courageous, not fearful. We must progress. We have to progress to fund public safety and infrastructure and education.

As I focus on natural resources, know that I won't overlook our greatest resource—our children. Our kids deserve the best in education. So, with fresh perspective in schools and K-12 putting parents back as the head of the education family, recognizing that they must guide children, empowering them via school involvement and choices. We can re-engage with prospects of success, and I know as a parent, as the guide, I know it's easier to say than to do—believe me.

I believe in public education. I'm proud of my family's many, many years working in our schools. I hope my claim to fame, believe it or not, is never that I'm Alaska's first female governor. I hope it continues to be, "You're Mr. Heath's daughter." My dad for years has been teaching in the schools and even today he's inspiring students across the state. So many students around this land came up to me not saying, "Oh, you're Sarah Palin...you're running for office...you're the governor." No, it's been, "Sarah Palin, wow! Mr. Heath's been my favorite teacher of all time."

Our teachers are our inspiration. We'll provide for successful public schools. I'll treat alternative schools with respect and with enthusiasm because, in fact, every child is worth it. We'll replicate winning reform so more kids are prepared for work, and we don't import our work force. Much reform won't cost more, it's a matter of priorities so more money gets into the classrooms. Our task is great but so worthy because I won't accept our 40 per cent high-school dropout rate, nor our lowest college-preparedness rate. That's not success. That's unacceptable. We must do better prioritizing. Students must be answerable and schools held accountable and our good teachers treasured for edifying our most precious resource, those kids. I'm excited to work with the schools to help each child find purpose and know their worth because everyone has great purpose. Getting kids on the right path, enabling them to be productive citizens—that's our goal together—in a safe environment.

That's another core constitutional intent—public safety. We've got to take it back and make every community safer and healthier. Preventing crime and substance abuse relates to family and culture strength and also depends on a vibrant economy. We know the positive effect of employment. It's been said that idle hands do the Devil's work. Well, to get idle hands to work, we teach, and through vo-tech training, we refill workforce deficits and we sway young Alaskans to stay and to improve themselves and to improve their state.

So, fifty years ago, this constitution captured a visionary dream filled with promise. Around this gift was a ribbon in the form of a resolution so relevant today. I was reminded this morning by President Hamilton of the University of Alaska as he shared what the resolution said.

It said, "You are Alaska's children. We bequeath you a state that shall be glorious in her achievements, a homeland filled with opportunity for a living, a land where you can worship and pray— an Alaska that will grow as you grow. We trust you. You are our future. Take tomorrow, and dream. You'll see visions that we do not see. We are certain that in capturing today for you, you can plan and build. Take our constitution. Study it. Work with it. Help others appreciate it. You are Alaska's children."

I accept this resolution on your behalf, on behalf of all Alaskans. Our sourdoughs and cheechakos, our proud military, our rugged hunters and outdoor enthusiasts, our academics and artisans, all who live in the last frontier and make it exceptional. For you, I rededicate support for our foundation.

I will defend our values. I'll show fiscal restraint to not burden our children with debt and deficit. I'll support competition and free enterprise. I'll insist on ethics in government. I will respect you. I will put Alaska first.

I ran for governor not thinking myself better than anyone, but offering opportunity for the mantle of leadership to be passed. It is time. That torch is fanned with new energy but was ignited long before by pioneers with a responsible, confident vision that I share. Its radiance won't let us lose sight of true north.

Alaskans, hold me accountable, and right back at you! I'll expect a lot from you, too. Take responsibility for your family and for your futures. Don't think you need government to take care of all needs and to make decisions for you. More government isn't the answer because you have ability, because you are Alaskans and you live in a land where God, with incredible benevolence, decided to overwhelmingly bless.

I'll help you with opportunities. I ask for your continued support in this for Lieutenant Governor Sean Parnell and me. And I ask that you join us in seeking God's wisdom, grace, and favor on Alaska. I thank you all and I thank my family for their amazing support and the responsibilities that they now have...girls? Thank you for sharing your mom—Bristol, Willow, and Piper—and our son Track who's outside playing hockey this year. I wish that he were in the Carlson today. Todd, thank you, I love you, thank you for everything.

Alaskans, I am grateful for you and for your warm heart. Alaska's new team cannot wait to get to work for you. We love Alaska, and God bless you all.

AUTHOR'S SOURCE NOTES

CHAPTER 1 GROWING UP SARAH

Interviews:
Chuck & Sally Heath. October 29, 2007, November 5, 2007
Heather Heath Bruce. October 30, 2007
Molly Heath McCann. November 3, 2007
Chuck Heath Jr. November 7, 2007, email & phone

CHAPTER 2 HEAVEN & HOOPS

Interviews:
Rev. Paul & Helen Riley. November 9, 2007
Don Teeguarden. November 3, 2007
Cordell Randall. November 10, 2007

Video. Alaska girl's state basketball championship, 1982, provided by Cordell Randall

Kizzia, Tom. "Fresh Face launched Palin," *Anchorage Daily News*, October 23, 2006

CHAPTER 3: SOMETHING ABOUT SARAH

Interviews:
Kim "Tilly" Ketchum. November 10, 2007
Helena "Lena" Andree. December 14, 2007
Sara & Todd Palin. December 11, 2007
Amy McCorkell. November 30, 2007

McAllister, Bill. "Tough Cookie," KTUU Capitol Ideas blog. http://www.ktuu.com/Global/story.asp?S=7310775, November 4, 2007

Chapter 4: Sarah Takes on City Hall

Interview:
Sara & Todd Palin. December 11, 2007

Holland, Megan. "Stevens explains email remarks—Valley Trash," *Anchorage Daily News.* July 29, 2004

Wasilla election results. City of Wasilla clerk's office

Staff. "Palin Challenges Stein in Wasilla," *Anchorage Daily News,* August 2, 1996

Lohman, Mike. "Letters to the editor: Palin will listen," *Frontiersman,* September 18, 1996

Mitchell Harris, Laura. "Wasilla mayoral candidates face off at chamber," *Frontiersman,* September 13, 1996

Mitchell Harris, Laura. "Campaign heats up," *Frontiersman,* September 25, 1996

Baugh, Dean; Cooper III, John P.; Emmons, Mary Ellen; Felton, John T.; Stambaugh, Irl T. "Letters to the editor: City responsive," *Frontiersman,* September 25, 1996

Komarnitsky, S.J. "Republicans draw fire for backing candidates in Mat-Su's elections," *Anchorage Daily News,* September 28, 1996

Komarnitsky, S.J. "Palin wins Wasilla mayor's job; Nolfi, Hartrick capture borough assembly seats," *Anchorage Daily News,* October 2, 1996

Komarnitsky, S.J. "New mayor, sharp knife; Wasilla winner says she'll halve taxes, take pay cut," *Anchorage Daily News,* October 3, 1996

Mitchell Harris, Laura. "Palin new Wasilla mayor," *Frontiersman,* October 4, 1996

Mitchell Harris, Laura. "Palin eager to take the helm at Wasilla City Hall," *Frontiersman,* October 11, 1996

Mitchell Harris, Laura. "Wasilla council gridlocked," *Frontiersman,* October 16, 1996

Mitchell Harris, Laura. "Wasilla council seats 2 members," *Frontiersman,* October 23, 1996

Mitchell Harris, Laura. "Palin: Ploy broke logjam," *Frontiersman,* October 25, 1996

Komarnitsky, S.J. "New Wasilla mayor asks city's manager to resign in loyalty test, *Anchorage Daily News,* October 26, 1996

Mitchell Harris, Laura. "Department heads fates uncertain," *Frontiersman,* October 30, 1996

Mitchell Harris, Laura. "Palin: new policy not gag order," *Frontiersman,* October 30, 1996

Komarnitsky, S. J. "Wasilla mayor fires police, library chiefs," *Anchorage Daily News,* January 31, 1997

Komarnitsky, S.J. "Wasilla keeps librarian, but police chief is out," *Anchorage Daily News,* February 1, 1997

Kormarnitsky, S.J. "Foes back off their push to recall mayor," *Anchorage Daily News,* February 11, 1997

Toomey, Sheila. "Firing suit in Wasilla hits court," *Anchorage Daily News,* February 22, 1997

Komarnitsky, S.J. "Judge backs Chief's firing; Wasilla mayor within rights," *Anchorage Daily News,* March 1, 2000

Komarnitsky, S.J. "Wasilla eliminates three taxes," *Anchorage Daily News,* December 24, 1997

Komarnitsky, S.J. "Mayoral race tests valley; Wasilla contest represents struggle to govern Mat-Su," *Anchorage Daily News,* September 20, 1999

Komarnitsky, S.J. "Peninsula, Mat-Su go to polls," *Anchorage Daily News,* October 5, 1999

Komarnitsky, S.J. "Palin wins re-election in Wasilla," *Anchorage Daily News,* October 6, 1999

CHAPTER 5: PLAYING IN THE BIG LEAGUES

Interviews:
Sara & Todd Palin. December 11, 2007
Judy Patrick. December 12, 2007

Willis Lyford. January 9, 2008
Pete Hallgren. December 10, 2007

Ruskin, Liz. "Murkowski says he will run for governor next year," *Anchorage Daily News*, October 23, 2001

Cockerham, Sean. "Fink touts Palin for lieutenant governor," *Anchorage Daily* News, July 28, 2002

Inklebarger, Timothy. "Republican political heavyweights battle for lt. governor spot," *Juneau Empire*, August 14, 2002

Cockerham, Sean. "Money flows in race for 2nd spot on ticket," *Anchorage Daily News*, August 11, 2002

Cockerham, Sean. "Candidates disagree on state fiscal gap," *Anchorage Daily News*, August 18, 2002

Cockerham, Sean. "The race for No. 2: GOP lieutenant governor candidates offer answers to key questions," *Anchorage Daily News*, August 21, 2002

Hunter, Don. "Ulmer, Murkowski grab leads; Leman: GOP voters tap retiring senator for lieutenant governor," *Anchorage Daily News*, August 28, 2002

Pemberton, Mary. "Leman wins close fight in lt. gov. race," Associated Press, posted on AlaskaLegislature.com. August 28, 2002

Ruskin, Liz. "Logistics behind appointing U.S. senator kindle debate," *Anchorage Daily News*, November 12, 2002

Ruskin, Liz. "Murkowski releases list of 25 potential replacements," *Anchorage Daily News,* November 16, 2002

Cockerham, Sean. "Senator quizzes 8-9 for seat; Murkowski: Governor-elect to name replacement by Dec. 9 or 10," *Anchorage Daily News*, November 22, 2002

Ruskin, Liz. "Mum's the word from Murkowski; rumors rule," *Anchorage Daily News,* December 4, 2002

Ruskin, Liz. "Murkowski Senate list cut to six," *Anchorage Daily News*, December 17, 2002

Cockerham, Sean. "Murkowski picks daughter to fill his U.S. Senate seat," *Anchorage Daily News*, December 21, 2002

Inklebarger, Timothy. "Initiative steeped in partisan battles; Senate vacancy measure would require a special election for an open seat," *Juneau Empire*, October 7, 2004

CHAPTER 6: PIT BULL IN LIPSTICK

Interviews:
Sarah Palin. December 27, 2007
Kathy Wells. December 15, 2007
Chris Wittington Evans. December 16, 2007
Eric Croft. December 20, 2007

Staff. "Opinion: Ruedrich emails," *Anchorage Daily News,* March 7, 2004

Mauer, Richard. "GOP chief settles, is fined; Randy Ruedrich: Party boss admits violations, to pay $12,000," *Anchorage Daily News*, June 23, 2004

Mauer, Richard. "Palin explains her actions in Ruedrich case; Ethics: Former oil and gas commissioner's missteps went beyond his partisan work," *Anchorage Daily News,* September 18, 2004

Dobbyn, Paula. "Renkes mixes personal, state business, *Anchorage Daily News*, December 5, 2004

Palin, Sarah. "Odd couple's motivation not political—Compass Points of view from the community," *Anchorage Daily News*, December 17, 2004

Cockerham, Sean. "Bundy in error, brief says; Complaint: Croft maintains ex-U.S. attorney misread ethics act during Renkes investigation," *Anchorage Daily News,* February 5, 2005

Volz, Matt. "Alaska Attorney General Gregg Renkes to resign," Associated Press, *USA Today,* February 6, 2005

Dobbyn, Paula. "Renkes settles ethics matter; Case: Ex-attorney general agrees to allow documents to be disclosed," *Anchorage Daily News*. March 9, 2005

Dobbyn, Paula. "Personnel board calls for ethics act revision; Renkes: Statement calls probe by Bundy appropriate," *Anchorage Daily News*, March 12, 2005

CHAPTER 7: FRANK MURKOWSKI'S DOWNFALL

Interview:
Karen Compton. January 3, 2008

Chambers, Mike. "Murkowski vows rebirth for state; Stars in alignment, governor says, with unity in Juneau, Washington," Associated Press, *Anchorage Daily News*, December 3, 2002

Brown, Cathy. "House refuses phase-out plan; longevity bonus: The issue could come up for vote again today," Associated Press, *Anchorage Daily News*, May 21, 2003

Inklebarger, Timothy. "Losing the longevity bonus: As deadline for last check approaches, seniors look for answers," *Juneau Empire*, July 17, 2003

Staff. "Alaska: Ban on Long-Term Senate Appointees," *New York Times*, June 10, 2004

Staff. "Governor's jet lands outside budget; No dice: Constituents don't buy plan to lease state aircraft, lawmakers say," *Anchorage Daily News*, February 19, 2005

Cockerham, Sean. "Jet plan will fly, Governor declares; Reaction: Lawmakers scoff but say Murkowski has authority to lease aircraft," *Anchorage Daily News*, April 21, 2005

Cockerham, Sean. "State's new jet upgraded, could touch down today; Turbulence: Critics have contended the $2.7 million plane isn't needed," *Anchorage Daily News*, November 8, 2005

Balz, Dan. "Alaska's governor may lose his job," *Washington Post*, August 22, 2006

Hopkins, Kyle. "Knowles, Palin in November," *Anchorage Daily News*, August 22, 2006

CHAPTER 8: A FAMILY DECISION

Interviews:
Sarah Palin. December 27, 2007
John Reeves. January 7, 2008
Willis Lyford. January 9, 2008

Cockerham, Sean. "Natural Resources Commissioner Irwin's gas-line memo has cost him his job," *Anchorage Daily News*, October 28, 2005

CHAPTER 9: A SIMPLE PROMISE

Interviews:
Kris & Clark Perry, Dorwin & Joanne Smith. December 1, 2007
Frank Bailey. December 11, 2007; January 7, 2008. Email correspondence December 11, 2007; February 3, 2008
Matthew Peters. December 19, 2007
Lydia Wirkus. December 22, 2007

KTUU-TV Republican Roundtable: 2006 Gubernatorial Debate, August 7, 2006

Staff. Alaska Ear, *Anchorage Daily News*, August 12, 2006

Coyne, Amanda. "Sarah Smile: Ms. Palin turns AK's GOP inside out," *Anchorage Press,* August 17-23, 2006

Hulen, Richard; Mauer, Rich. "The Alaska political corruption investigation," adn.com posted December 7, 2007. http://community.adn.com/adn/node112569

Kizzia, Tom. "Is oil-tax taint real, or did PPT pass fairly?" *Anchorage Daily News*, October 28, 2007.

CHAPTER 10: ELECTION 2006

Interviews:
Sean Parnell. December 11, 2007
Bill McAllister. November 27, 2007; January 8, 2008
Kerm Ketchum. January 4, 2008

Anchorage Rotary gubernatorial debate, October 31, 2006

Dan Fagan KFQD-AM talk radio program, November 1, 2006

Alaska Gubernatorial Tracking Survey. Dittman Research & Communications, August-November 2006

Chapter 11 : For such a time as this

Interviews:
Katie Hurley. January 24, 2008
Wendy Garwood. January 24, 2008
Nick Timurphy. January 8, 2008
Curtis & Linda Menard. January 1, 2008

"The 49th Star" documentary. KUAC TV, University of Alaska Fairbanks, 2006

Milkowski, Stefan. "Gov. Palin takes office; Fairbanks hosts first inauguration outside Juneau since statehood," *Fairbanks Daily News-Miner*, December 5, 2006

Pemberton, Mary. "Palin steps in to 'guard' the state," Associated Press, AlaskaLegislature.com, posted December 5, 2006

Inaugural speech. Governor Sarah Palin, Fairbanks, Alaska, December 4, 2006

Inaugural speech. Lieutenant Governor Sean Parnell, Fairbanks, Alaska, December 4, 2006

Epilogue

Haycox, Steve. "Palin interview bolsters positive image," *Anchorage Daily News*, September 2, 2007

Hopkins, Kyle. "Euphoria turns to work for Palin; Difficult job forging administration looms," *Anchorage Daily News,* November 9, 2006

Hopkins, Kyle. "Inaugural eve—with campaign over, Palin government takes shape; New governor takes office Monday," *Anchorage Daily News,* December 3, 2006

Sutton, Anne. "Palin to examine last-hour job blitz; Murkowski: His ex-staff chief was appointed to a gas pipeline authority he bucked," Associated Press, *Anchorage Daily News*, December 6, 2006

Hopkins, Kyle. "Governor's jet to be sold on eBay; Westwind II: The plane became a point of ridicule against ex-Gov. Murkowski," *Anchorage Daily News*, December 13, 2006

Holland, Megan. "Company off hook thanks to pardon; Family stunned; Man was killed in avalanche near Cordova in 1999," *Anchorage Daily News*, December 24, 2006

Quinn, Steve. "Pardons mandate advising victims—Legislation: Action by former Gov. Murkowski drove the new law," *Anchorage Daily News,* February 21. 2007

Parnell, Sean. "My turn: Turn the private sector loose," *Juneau Empire*, April 30, 2007

Ayres, Sabra. "Alaska's governor tops the charts—89-93 poll ratings: Palin has pleased most voters by sticking to her promises," *Anchorage Daily News*, May 30, 2007

Halpin, James. "Dairy bailout called wrong business plan; Failure: Some experts see rescue as 'poor use of funds' by state," *Anchorage Daily News*, June 22, 2007

Halpin, James. "Palin signs ethics reforms; Law closes loopholes, stipulates bans as legislative cleanup begins state lawmakers to face new rules," *Anchorage Daily News,* July 10, 2007

Kizzia, Tom. "Palin foresees positive changes in Alaska politics," three-part series, *Anchorage Daily News*, September 2, 3, 4, 2007

Governor's office press release. "Gravina access project redirected," September 27, 2007

Breslau, Karen. "Now this is women's work," *Newsweek*, October 15, 2007

Forgey, Pat. "Legislature OKs oil tax hike: Bipartisan effort, with help of Juneau delegation, hands Palin an improbable victory," *Juneau Empire*, November 18, 2007

McAllister, Bill. "Palin outlines plan for surplus," KTUU-TV broadcast and web post. http://www.ktuu.com/Global/story.asp?s=7457957, December 6, 2007

DeVaugh, Melissa. "Palin's Way," *Alaska* magazine, February, 2008

Johnson, Rebecca. "Sarah Palin: An Alaskan Straight shooter is determined to fight corruption," *Vogue* magazine, February, 2008

INDEX

ABOUT THE AUTHOR

Kaylene Johnson is a writer and long-time Alaskan who makes her home on a small farm outside Wasilla. She enjoys hiking, skiing, and horseback riding in the backcountry. She is married with two sons and two grandsons. Her award-winning articles have appeared in *Alaskan Wilderness Discovery Guide, Alaska* magazine, the *Los Angeles Times, Spirit* magazine, and other publications. She received a BA from Vermont College and holds an MFA in Writing from Spalding University in Louisville, Kentucky.

RECOMMENDATIONS FOR READERS
seeking to learn more about Alaska and
its culture and history through biographies and memoirs
of notable Alaskans.

ACCIDENTALADVENTURER
Memoir of the First Woman to Climb
Mt. McKinley
BARBARA WASHBURN, PAPERBACK,
$16.95

ALASKA BLUES
A Story of Freedom, Risk, and Living
Your Dream
JOE UPTON, PAPERBACK, $14.95

ARCTIC BUSH PILOT
From Navy Combat to Flying Alaska's
Northern Wilderness
JAMES "ANDY" ANDERSON & JIM
REARDEN, PAPERBACK, $17.95

GEORGE CARMACK
Man of Mystery Who Set off the
Klondike Gold Rush
JAMES ALBERT JOHNSON,
PAPERBACK, $14.95

NORTH TO WOLF COUNTRY
My Life among the Creatures
of Alaska
JAMES W. BROOKS, PAPERBACK,
$16.95

ON THE EDGE OF NOWHERE
JIM HUNTINGTON & LAWRENCE
ELLIOTT, PAPERBACK, $14.95

ONE SECOND TO GLORY
The Alaska Adventures of Iditarod
Champion Dick Mackey
LEW FREEDMAN, PAPERBACK,
$16.95

RAISING OURSELVES
A Gwitch'in Coming of Age Story from
the Yukon River
VELMA WALLIS, PAPERBACK,
$14.95

SELLING ALASKA
A Pioneer Advertising Man's White
Collar Adventures
KAY GUTHRIE, PAPERBACK,
$14.95

SISTERS
Coming of Age & Living Dangerously
in the Wild Copper River Valley
SAMME GALLAHER & AILEEN
GALLAHER, PAPERBACK,
$14.95

TALES OF ALASKA'S
BUSH RAT GOVERNOR
The Extraordinary Autobiography of
Jay Hammond, Wilderness Guide and
Reluctant Politician
JAY HAMMOND, PAPERBACK,
$17.95

These titles can be found at or special-ordered
from your local bookstore. A wide assortment of
Alaska books also can be ordered directly from the
publisher's website, www.EpicenterPress.com,
or by calling 1-800-950-6663 anytime day or night.

EPICENTER PRESS / ALASKA BOOK ADVENTURES™
WWW.EPICENTERPRESS.COM